A DUTY TO OFFEND:

SELECTED ESSAYS

BY BRENDAN O'NEILL

A DUTY TO OFFEND:

SELECTED ESSAYS

BY BRENDAN O'NEILL

Connor Court Publishing

Connor Court Publishing Pty Ltd

Copyright © Brendan O'Neill 2015

PO Box 224W

Ballarat VIC 3350

sales@connorcourt.com

www.connorcourt.com

ISBN: 9781925138764 (pbk.)

Cover design by Maria Giordano

Printed in Australia

CONTENTS

1. DRUNK SEX

Is it acceptable to have drunk sex? Most people who aren't citizens of the Islamic State or inhabitants of a nunnery will answer with an emphatic: 'Hell, yeah.' Not only is it acceptable, they'll think; it's good, one of life's great pleasures, a rare moment when you can ditch the pesky rational thinking required in everyday life and instead abandon yourself—mind, soul, and genitals—to a moment of dumb, beautiful joy.

Well, enjoy it while you can, folks. Because like everything else pleasurable in the 21st century—smoking in a bar, complimenting a lady on her looks, drinking a bucket-sized Coke—drunk sex is under attack from that new caste of killjoys who wouldn't recognise fun if it offered to buy them a drink ('unwanted sexual advance'). Drunk sex is being demonised, even criminalised, turned from something that can be either wonderful or awkward into, effectively, rape. They warned us for years, 'Don't drink and drive'. Now it's, 'Don't drink and fuck'.

Alison Saunders, Britain's Director of Public Prosecutions, the boss lady of all the British state's legal actions against suspected lawbreakers, has issued new advice on rape. Sent to cops around Britain as part of a 'toolkit' of tips for dealing with rape cases, it says society must move 'beyond the old saying "no means no"'. Because apparently women are sometimes incapable of saying no when they would probably like to. When? When they're shit-faced, as Americans say; or pissed as a fart, as us Brits prefer.

'It is not a crime to drink', said Saunders (she might have added a 'yet', because I'm sure some teetoaller in the corridors of British power is working on this), but it is a crime 'to target someone who is no longer capable of consenting to sex through drink', she continued. And she wants the law to be better able to deal with what the press has called those 'grey areas' (*50 Shades of Grey* areas?) in which sex happens when someone is 'incapacitated through drink or drugs'. Her advice to cops and lawyers is that in every case of allegedly dodgy, drunk, disputed sex, they should demand of the suspect: 'How did [you] know the complainant was saying yes and doing so freely and knowingly?'

There are many terrifying things about this advice. The first is its subtle shifting of the burden of proof so that it falls to the defendant to prove that the claimant said 'yes' rather than to the claimant to prove she said 'no' and was ignored. As Sarah Vine of the *Daily Mail* says, this could lead to a situation where 'men in rape cases [will] automatically be presumed guilty until they can prove they obtained consent'. In essence, this would mean sex becoming default a crime until you, the drunk dude who slept with the drunk girl, can prove that your sex wasn't malevolent. Imagine raising such an idea in the year in which we celebrate the 800th anniversary of Magna Carta, midwife of the presumption of innocence, which for centuries guarded citizens from the whims and prejudices of the mighty state and powerful prosecutors like Ms Saunders.

But even worse is her thought-free mash-up of drunk sex and rape, as if they're the same. When Saunders talks about sex that happens while one or both parties is hammered, she's sticking her snout—the state's snout—into what for many people is a perfectly normal part of life: college parties, house parties, youthful get-togethers, at which the truly shocking thing would be to see sober people getting it on.

She's following the lead of today's campus killjoys: the Orwellian junior sex leagues masquerading as feminists who for a decade have been turning student sex into something foul and potentially criminal.

On both sides of the Atlantic, campuses that were once hotbeds of anti-The Man radicalism have become conveyor belts of conformist policymaking, particularly in relation to anything that has what these prudish heirs to Andrea Dworkin consider to be the rancid whiff of s*x. And what kind of sex do they loathe most? Drunk sex.

Numerous colleges now insist that it isn't possible to consent to sex if you're three sheets to the wind, which means that all sexual acts carried out under the influence are potential crimes. The University of Georgia warns students that sexual consent must be 'voluntary, sober, imaginative, enthusiastic, creative, wanted, informed, mutual, honest'. There are many problematic words in that—'imaginative'? Can't we consent to sex unimaginatively, maybe by saying 'Oh, go on then'?—but the most problematic is 'sober'. Apparently sex must always be booze-free.

These consent commandments are found on campuses across the West. At Oxford and Cambridge in the UK, sexual-consent classes are now compulsory for all first-year students. (Compulsory classes on consent? What delicious, Orwellian irony.) At these classes, students are told they must be of 'sound and sober mind' to consent to sex. So, no paralytic, sozzled, WTF sex.

The University of Wyoming takes this authoritarian downer on drunk sex to its logical conclusion by warning students: 'Sex that occurs while a partner is intoxicated or high is not consensual ... it is sexual assault.' If this stipulation were enforced retroactively, pretty much every person I went to university with could be arrested for rape. Everyone had a blind-drunk bang at some point, because it was fun.

Some of the sex-scared authoritarianism on campus merely mirrors shifts in certain states' law, where intoxication is increasingly said to void consent. But elsewhere, the student anti-sex leagues are helping to reshape the law, as can be seen in Saunders' enthusiastic embrace of the idea that drunk sex is A Very Bad Thing.

It's hard to know what is most repulsive about this creeping criminalisation of inebriated fornication. Is it the way it infantilises women with its sexist implication that they are less capable of negotiating sexual encounters while drunk than men, hence the drunk man must shoulder responsibility for these apparently depraved shenanigans? This echoes the temperance movements of the late 19th century, which likewise warned dainty ladies that getting blotto would lead to sexual misadventure and downfall. Or is it the way it demonises men, turning even the sweet, utterly non-violent young lad who has to have eight vodkas to buck up the courage to sleep with his beau into that most heinous of criminals: a rapist? Or is it the fact that its aim is to deprive us of one of the great hoots of human life: stupid sex, where you don't know, or care, what is going on, where the condom is, or even if she's on the Pill? That moment of madness, that instant when feeling takes over and your brain has a night off, that time when you can't string a sentence together but somehow you can still have sex… seriously, students, you should try this.

The big problem is the shift in recent years from talking about rape to 'sex without consent'. Rape is a violent word that describes a conscious act by a wicked man (usually) to defy a woman who says no and to force sex on her. Disgusting. Lock him up. But 'sex without consent' is a totally different phrase: it's more passive, signalling an act that doesn't require criminal intent and which can cover everything from rape as it was once understood to drunk sex, drugged-up sex, or regretted sex. We've gone from punishing those who rape to casting a vast blanket of suspicion over anyone who has sex. But the fact is—and please don't hate me—sex isn't always 100 per cent consensual. Especially after booze. Sometimes it's instinctual, thoughtless, animalistic. Sometimes it just happens. It's sex without consent—that is, without explicit, clearly stated, sober consent—but it ain't rape. It's sex.

The cultivation of the new crime of 'sex without consent' completes the state's intervention into private life. It effectively makes the authorities into the arbiters of sex itself, the judges of when sex is okay and when it isn't, of whether a particular drunken romp is acceptable or rape. Don't drink and fuck, or the state will fuck you—with or without your consent.

Reason, 1 March 2015

2. MARXISTS FOR CAPITALISM

As someone who still considers himself a Marxist—I know: crazy, right?—I guess I should feel angry about reckless, risk-hungry bankers. Yet I find myself in the curious position today of thinking capitalism isn't risk-hungry enough, certainly in areas where it matters: developing the forces of production and creating new wealth. I also find myself shaking my head in violent disagreement whenever I hear so-called radicals put the boot into capitalism. They seem to loathe the very parts of the capitalist system Marx quite liked. Help! I'm a Marxist who defends capitalism.

It's trendy to be an anti-capitalist these days. Newspaper columnists attack greedy fat-cats and their big bonuses. Environmentalists protest about the impact of the capitalists' dirty factories and aeroplane-enabled international trade on poor Mother Earth, where it's not so much a case of everything solid melting into air, as Marx described the rise of the bourgeoisie, but everything solid polluting the air, with smog and soot and various other godless toxins. Some posh kids born with an entire cutlery set of silver in their mouths now stop washing their hair in order to develop dreadlocks and then wield cudgels against a McDonald's restaurant or a Starbucks outlet. Meanwhile, everyone looks at China as it lumbers from Maoism to capitalism, building a mind-boggling two coal-fired power stations every week, and says in unison: 'Eurgh!'

Marx would have told these shallow anti-capitalists to get a grip. Where they view capitalists as overly cocky and arrogant, always erecting new factories and building new cities to satisfy mankind's insatiable lust for stuff, Marx was quite happy to champion the naked ambition of the capitalist class. In *The Communist Manifesto*, Marx and his sidekick Friedrich Engels upheld and even celebrated the achievements of capitalism in overcoming and controlling nature, through its rapid development of industry, science, agriculture and telecommunications. The capitalist class was the first in history, said Marx and Engels, to 'show what man's activity can bring about'. In only a century, it had 'accomplished wonders far surpassing Egyptian pyramids, Roman aqueducts and Gothic cathedrals; it has conducted expeditions that put in the shade all former exoduses of nations and crusades'. These days, the 'wonders' of modern capitalism—whether it's the 4×4 or digital TV or genetically modified crops—are more likely to be looked upon as wicked things that corrupt nature rather than as wonderful things that liberate humanity. It is striking that, today, well-off newspaper columnists and the spoilt-brat sons and daughters of the aristocracy and other money-lubed sections of society are unwilling to defend the kind of capitalist gains that even communists were celebrating more than 150 years ago.

Today's capitalist-bashers also dislike international trade and development, especially since it involves flying products around the world, which leaves a long, streaking carbon skidmark in the skies. Environmentalists bang on about the problem of 'food miles'—the distance grub travels before it reaches our plates—and even 'love miles', the bloody killjoys, which refers to the distance your red roses and boxes of Belgian chocolates travel before you hand them, like an unthinking slave to capitalist desire, to your loved one. New movements celebrate local production over international trade: the Oxford American Dictionary's word of the year was 'locavore', which refers to a new breed of green-leaning Westerner who only eats food grown or harvested within 100 miles of where he or she lives. Meanwhile, Naomi Klein, queen of the anti-capitalists, writes tear-drenched tirades against the spread of capitalism into every corner of the globe, while eco-commentators celebrate the virtues of those few remaining tribes that have remained relatively capitalism-free.

Yet Marx quite admired the internationalising tendencies of the capitalist system. He argued that, 'to the chagrin of reactionists', capitalism dislodges local and national industries and turns production into a global phenomenon. 'The bourgeoisie, by the rapid improvement of all instruments of production, by the immensely facilitated means of communication, draws all, even the most barbarian, nations into civilisation', he and Engels wrote. Now, if you will forgive their 19th-century language, inappropriate and un-PC, I know, their point is clear: globalisation at least has the benefit of smashing down silly local practices and 'civilising' formerly backward societies. What's more, this opens up the potential for a truly universal culture, said the communist duo: 'The intellectual creations of individual nations become common property. National one-sidedness and narrow-mindedness become more and more impossible, and from the numerous national and local literatures, there arises a world literature.'

Hurrah! Only today's lazy anti-capitalists—locavores and reactionists the lot of them—celebrate the local over the international, and fight to preserve one-sided and narrow-minded cultural practices around the world from what they see as the carbon bootprint of capitalist expansionism. Unlike Marx, they're not interested in superseding capitalism with something better— with something even more global and more productive, which will leave an even bigger human footprint on the planet—but rather in returning to a pre-capitalist era of local food production, dancing around maypoles and early death from cholera or malnutrition.

What today's anti-capitalists loathe most is the 'consumer society', with its incessant advertising and wicked temptation to buy, buy, buy. On Buy Nothing Day recently, anti-capitalist protesters on Oxford Street, London and elsewhere advised shoppers to 'detox from consumerism' because 'everything we buy has an impact on our planet'. Meanwhile, serious psychologists (as well as the seriously psychotic) claim consumerism makes us ill—it gives us 'affluenza', apparently. Geddit?

Marx loved the consumer society. Indeed, he described it as a 'civilising moment' of capital. In the Grundrisse, he wrote: 'In spite of all his "pious" speeches, [the capitalist] searches for means to spur [the workers] on to consumption, to give his wares new charms, to inspire them with new needs by constant chatter, etc. It is precisely this side of the relation of capital and labour which is an essential civilising moment.' It is striking that what a bearded communist described as 'civilising' 150 years ago—the chatter and charms of consumerism—is now written off by anti-capitalists as dangerous and corrupting.

Of course, Marx wanted to destroy capitalism because he thought it didn't go far enough in remaking the world in man's image and organising society according to man's needs and desires. Today's sorry excuses for Marxists and anti-capitalists think capitalism has gone too far in its development of the forces of production and encouragement of consumerism. I'm with Marx. Let's replace capitalism with something even more dazzlingly cocky and human-centric. But first let's deal with the luddites, locavores and eco-feudalists who have given anti-capitalism a bad name.

The Spectator, 28 November 2007

3. Bringing Spinoza back

'Every man should think what he likes and say what he thinks.' It is 350 years since Spinoza, the great Dutchman of the Enlightenment, wrote those simple but profound words. And yet every man (and woman) is still not at liberty to think what he likes, far less say it. We must breathe life back into the Spinoza spirit, make the case anew for allowing everyone to say what he thinks, as honestly and frankly as he likes.

It is true that, unlike in Spinoza's day, no one in the 21st century is dragged to 'the scaffold' and 'put to death' for saying out loud what lurks in his heart—at least not in the West. But right now, right here, in the apparently democratic West, people are being arrested, fined, shamed, censored, cut off, cast out of polite society, and even jailed for the supposed crime of thinking what they like and saying what they think. You might not be hanged by the neck for speaking your mind, but you do risk being hung out to dry, by coppers, the courts, censorious Twittermobs and other self-elected guardians of the allegedly right way of thinking and correct way of speaking.

Ours is an age in which a pastor, in Sweden, can be sentenced to a month in jail for preaching to his own flock in his own church that homosexuality is a sin. In which British football fans can be arrested for referring to themselves as 'Yids'. In which French people who have too stingingly criticised the Islamic ritual slaughter of animals have been convicted of committing a hate crime. In which Britain's leading liberal writers and arts people can, *sans* shame, put their names to a letter calling for state regulation of the press, the very scourge their cultural forebears risked their heads fighting against. In which students in Britain, America and Australia have become bizarrely ban-happy, censoring songs, newspapers and speakers that rile their minds. In which offence-taking has become the central organising principle of much of the political sphere, nurturing virtual gangs of the ostentatiously outraged who swarm on Twitter to demand, often successfully, the purging from public life of any article, advert or argument that upsets them—a modern-day version of what Spinoza called 'quarrelsome mobs', the 'real disturbers of the peace'.

Freedom of speech is in a bad way. Yes, politicians pay lip service to it; the EU celebrates it as a core Euro-value; constitutions guaranteeing it abound on campuses. But in everyday life, in the real, rowdy public square, in the actual, psychical academy, political world and sphere of publishing, freedom of speech is increasingly treated as a negotiable commodity, something that can be qualified by all sorts of rules, regulations or—a modern favourite—'responsibilities'. So the EU proudly trumpets its commitment to freedom of speech but then says this freedom can be curtailed by various 'formalities, conditions, restrictions and penalties'. Someone needs to buy the Brussels brigade a dictionary so that they might look up what the word freedom means. Those who want to speak freely might not be killed by the hangman anymore; but their liberty, their thoughts and ideas, are too often killed with qualifications.

The lack of a serious, deep commitment to freedom of speech is generating new forms of intolerance. And not just religious intolerance of the blasphemous, though that undoubtedly still exists (adverts in Europe have been banned for upsetting Christians and books in Britain and America have been shelved for fear that they might offend Muslims). We also have new forms of secular intolerance, with British government scientists calling for 'gross intolerance' of those who promote medical quackery, and serious magazines proposing the imprisonment of those who 'deny' climate change. Just as you can't yell fire in a crowded theatre, so you shouldn't be free to 'yell balderdash at 10,883 scientific journal articles a year, all saying the same thing', said the hip online magazine *Gawker* recently. In other words, thou shalt not blaspheme against the eco-gospel. Where once mankind struggled hard for the right to ridicule religious truths, now we must fight equally hard for the right to shout balderdash at climate-change theories, and any other modern orthodoxy that winds us up, makes us mad, or which we just don't like the sound of.

People with the 'wrong' views are being silenced, sometimes by the law, sometimes by the mob; sometimes by jail time, sometimes under pressure to conform, to recant their apparently ridiculous views on anything from global warming to gay marriage and effectively to allow their minds to 'lie wholly at the disposition of another', as Spinoza described earlier attempts to stifle free thought in favour of imposing orthodox non-thinking. This new censoriousness is bad for two reasons. First, because it prevents people from saying what they think, from expressing in a public forum their beliefs or ideas or plain old prejudices, which it should be everybody's right in a free, democratic society to do. And secondly because it prevents the rest of us, the potential audience to the silenced speech, from making up our minds about what is true and good, and what isn't. It makes us effectively into child-like charges of the state or some other body of the self-righteous, who have assumed the authority to think on our behalf, to decide on our behalf what is right, and therefore can be published, and to decide on our behalf what is wrong, and thus must be silenced.

The new illiberalism commits the double offence of shutting up those who have something to say and shutting down the critical faculties of everyone else. It gags the controversially inclined and weakens the moral muscles of the rest of us, the public, who ought to be as free to hear, and to pass judgement, as the writer or artist or rabble-rouser should be free to speak. The most immediate impact of censorship is its hushing of an individual who wants to utter something, but its more insidious impact is to infantilise society, to discourage thoughtfulness in favour of allowing us to consume only ideas that the great, good and influential have predetermined to be right, true, scientifically or politically correct, safe for us to imbibe.

We need a new fight for freedom of speech. We need a renewed commitment to the freedoms of thought, conscience, speech and the press, and one which is consistent—which defends these freedoms not only for intellectuals and the right-on, as too many free-speech campaign groups narrowly devote themselves to doing, but also for so-called deniers, for the politically weird, for those who are offensive or outrageous or disturbing. For it is only by having unfettered free speech that we can guarantee an open and lively public sphere in which bad claims or ideas might be beaten, and the truth, a real truth, arrived at.

Some people say freedom of speech is more complicated than people like me appreciate. But it really isn't. It's possibly the most straightforward of political issues. It is this simple: everyone should be free to think what he likes and say what he thinks, with no if, buts, erming, ahhing, restrictions, restraints or delay. Seriously: none.

spiked, 2 April 2014

4. DRINKS WITH BRANDIS

Ever since Captain Cook set foot here, Australia's exotic creatures have wowed the rest of the world. Mammals that lay eggs! Marsupials that hop! Well today, Australia contains what must surely count as the most exotic, rarely sighted creature of the 21st century: a politician who believes in freedom of speech. Extinct in Europe, seriously endangered in America, this most hunted of the modern era's political beasts still survives Down Under, and it goes by the name of George Brandis.

'I'm a John Stuart Mill man', Brandis tells me, over too much booze and amazing food at one of Sydney's oldest political haunts, which is called—wait for it—Machiavelli's. Brandis is the senator for Queensland for the ruling right-wing Liberal Party, a key cog in the government of Liberal PM Tony Abbott, and, most importantly, the attorney general of Australia. This basically means he's in charge of Australian law and justice. And since taking office with the election of Abbott in 2013, Brandis has doggedly, and often controversially, devoted himself to reforming the section of the Oz *Racial Discrimination Act* that forbids people from 'offending, insulting or humiliating' a person or group on the basis of their racial or ethnic origins. Why has he done this? Why is he so determined to rip up restrictions on insulting ethnic minorities? Why has he allowed himself to be branded by many on the Australian left as a 'friend of bigots' who is using his power to help 'unleash Australia's racists'?

'Because', he says, 'if you are going to defend freedom of speech, you have to defend the right of people to say things you would devote your political life to opposing. Your good faith is tested by whether or not you would defend the right to free speech of people with whom you profoundly disagree. That's the test.'

In an era when European politicians are forever battling it out to see who can outlaw the most forms of 'hate speech', when Canada hauls so-called hate speakers before its Human Rights Commission to justify themselves, when students in America and Britain ban, burn or no-platform anything they decree to be hateful—whether it's Zionist politicians or the pop super-hit 'Blurred Lines'— Brandis's single-minded campaign to rein in Australia's hate-speech laws is quite something. In fact it feels positively weird to hear a mainstream politician, someone whose face you see in the papers and on TV all the time here, talk about the 'limits of the state to interfere with the utterance of ideas, beliefs and opinions', and even to say, as Brandis does to me, that 'people have the right to be bigots, you know'. Try to imagine a British politician campaigning for, effectively, the freedom to hate; it just wouldn't happen.

Brandis says he's been a fan of free speech for ages. He reminds me that in his maiden speech to the Australian Senate, given 14 years ago when he was first elected as senator for Queensland, he let everyone know that 'one of my most fundamental objectives would be to protect freedom of thought and expression'. He tells me he has long been agitated by 'the cultural tyranny of political correctness'. But there were two things in particular that made him realise just what a mortal threat freedom of speech faces in the modern era and that he would have to dust down his Mill, reread his Voltaire, and up the ante in his war of words against, as he puts it, the transformation of the state into 'the arbiter of what might be thought'. The first thing was the climate-change debate; the second was the Andrew Bolt case.

He describes the climate-change debate—or non-debate, or anti-debate, to be really pedantic but also accurate—as one of the 'great catalysing moments' in his views about the importance of free speech. He isn't a climate-change denier; he says he was 'on the side of those who believed in anthropogenic global warming and who believed something ought to be done about it'. But he has nonetheless found himself 'really shocked by the sheer authoritarianism of those who would have excluded from the debate the point of view of people who were climate-change deniers'. He describes as 'deplorable' the way climate change has become a gospel truth that you deny or mock at your peril, 'where one side [has] the orthodoxy on its side and delegitimises the views of those who disagree, rather than engaging with them intellectually and showing them why they are wrong'

He describes how Penny Wong, the Labor Party senator for South Australia and minister for climate change in the Julia Gillard government, would 'stand up in the Senate and say "The science is settled". In other words, "I am not even going to engage in a debate with you". It was ignorant, it was medieval, the approach of these true believers in climate change.' Wong, whom Brandis tells me is 'Australia's high priestess of political correctness', is far from alone in suffering from what the American journalist Joel Kotkin describes as 'The Debate Is Over' Syndrome. Throughout eco-circles, and among the political and media elites more broadly, the idea that the time for debating climate change is over, and now we just need action, action, action, is widespread. And to Brandis, this speaks to a new and illiberal climate of anti-intellectualism, to the emergence of 'a habit of mind and mode of discourse which would deny the legitimacy of an alternative point of view, where rather than winning the argument [they] exclude their antagonists from the argument'.

The great irony to this new 'habit of mind', he says, is that the eco-correct think of themselves as enlightened and their critics as 'throwbacks', when actually 'they themselves are the throwbacks, because they adopt this almost theological view, this cosmology that eliminates from consideration the possibility of an alternative opinion'. The moral straitjacketing of anyone who raises a critical peep about eco-orthodoxies is part of a growing 'new secular public morality', he says, 'which seeks to impose its views on others, even at the cost of political censorship'.

The second thing that made him sharpen his pen and open his gob about the importance of free speech was the case of Andrew Bolt.

Bolt is one of Australia's most widely read journalists. He writes a column for the *Herald Sun* in Melbourne. He riles the hell out of lefties and people who work at the ABC. For British readers, think Richard Littlejohn, but better-read and more cultured. In 2010, he wrote some blog posts for the *Herald Sun* website criticising the fashion among 'fair-skinned people' to claim Aboriginal heritage, under the headlines: 'It's so hip to be black', 'White is the New Black' and 'White Fellas in the Black'. He was sued by nine individuals and was hauled off to court, where he was found to have contravened Section 18C of the *Racial Discrimination Act*—the bit that forbids 'offending, insulting or humiliating' ethnic groups. In a 57,000-word ruling, the judge said Bolt's articles were 'insulting', causing a 'loss of esteem' among the people criticised in them, and also slammed 'the manner in which the articles were written' and their 'inflammatory and provocative language'. The *Herald Sun* was forced by the court to publish a notice declaring that publication of the articles had been 'unlawful'.

Brandis is stinging about this case. The judge 'engaged in an act of political censorship', he says, with a journalist 'prohibited from expressing a point of view'. The reason Brandis is so keen to ditch the bit of the Racial Discrimination Act that allowed such a flagrant act of ideological censure to take place in 21st-century Australia is because while it is justified as a guard against outbursts of dangerous racism, actually it allows the state to police and punish legitimate public speech and debate. 'And the moment you establish the state as the arbiter of what might be said, you establish the state as the arbiter of what might be thought, and you are right in the territory that George Orwell foreshadowed', he says

So currently, Brandis is on a mission to reform Section 18C. He wants to remove the words 'insult', 'offend' and 'humiliate', but he is willing to leave in the stipulation against 'intimidation' of a person or group on the basis of their ethnic origins. He's receiving colossal flak from Australia's chattering classes. They accuse him of standing up for bigots. He didn't help himself when he said in the Senate a couple of weeks ago that people do have the right to be bigots. That unleashed a tsunami of ridicule, even from some of his supporters. But he tells me he has no regrets. 'I don't regret saying that because in this debate, sooner or later—and better sooner than later—somebody had to make the Voltaire point; somebody had to make the point [about] defending the right to free speech of people with whom you profoundly disagree.'

Brandis says there are two reasons he's bent on overhauling Section 18C. The first is because it expands the authority of the state into the realm of thought, where it should never tread, he says. 'There is a deeper question here, about the role of the state. To what extent should the state be the arbiter of what people can think? Now of course, the state is the arbiter of what people can do. The state, to use the most straightforward example imaginable, prohibits murder. It is the role of government to protect the weak from the strong. But this is about whether it is the role of government to tell people what they may think. In my view, freedom of speech, by which I mean the freedom to express and articulate beliefs and opinions, is a necessary and essential precondition of political freedom.'

And the second reason he wants Section 18C massively trimmed is because he believes censorship is the worst possible tool for tackling backward thinking. 'As you know, Brendan, John Stuart Mill, particularly in chapter 2 of *On Liberty*, made the case better than anyone has made it before or since that the best way for the public to be enlightened, for wicked opinions to be exposed for what they are, is to get them out in the cold light of day and let there be a contest of ideas. Let people judge, having heard the contest of ideas, what views are right and supportable, and what views are wrong.

'It is much better that we arrive at a community position on difficult social issues that way than some bureaucrat or human-rights commissioner or politician or public servant tells us what we're allowed to think and say. Political censorship is always wrong, not just because it is an assault on liberty, but because it is actually ineffective. The best way to popularise a political opinion is to censor it!'

In short, he wants restrictions on speech lifted because they both prevent people from expressing themselves and also rob the public of the right to discuss and pass judgement on various ideas; because they both censor the individual and disempower the demos. I'm with him. It remains to be seen how successful his agitation against the worst parts of Section 18C will be—the pressure on him to shelve his plans is intense.

As befits a Liberal attorney general who loathes PC, Brandis is scathing about the left. And that's understandable. After all, what passes for the left in modern Australia, in both journalism and campaigning circles, has been angrily slamming as dangerous and bigoted his plans to reform Section 18C, with *Guardian Australia* (yep, they're down here now) accusing him of 'giving racists a free rein'. 'The left has embraced a new authoritarianism', he says. 'Having abandoned the attempt to control the commanding heights of the economy, they now want to control the commanding heights of opinion, and that is even more dangerous.'

However, he's sussed enough to know that this is something new, that the left's turn against freedom of speech is a pretty recent thing: 'It's a complete inversion. The right, until maybe the 1970s or 80s, used to be on the side of censorship, and the left used to be on the side of liberation. That has inverted in the last 20 or 30 years. Now it is the left, in the name of political correctness, in the name of this kind of new secular public morality, which seeks to impose its views on others, even at the cost of political censorship. And it is the right, traditionally more authoritarian than the left, which has become the custodian of classical liberalism.

'The idea of there being a public morality which the state should at least endorse, if not enforce, used to be associated with the Tory point of view. The idea of non-conformism and free speech used to be associated with the left, and particularly the radical left. Now, the left has adopted a reasonably comprehensive secular morality of its own, which it now seeks to impose upon society. And it's prepared to impose that secular morality on society at the cost of the freedom of speech it once espoused. So there has been a very profound change in intellectual history in our lifetimes.'

Brandis is generous enough to recognise that 'most of the great social causes in the years since the Second World War were led by the left'. 'Women's liberation, gay liberation, wars of national liberation in the Third World—the language was the language of enlarging freedom, for oppressed groups or individuals or countries.' But now, he says, 'the left has abandoned the discourse of liberation … because they have a new construct which is all to do with power relationships in society. They are so concerned with rearranging power relationships, so as to disempower the empowered and elevate the disempowered, that they are prepared in the service of that end to sacrifice liberty. Nowadays, they regard liberty as the defence mechanism of the empowered.'

Indeed, in a recent TV discussion here about Section 18C, one firebrand leftist described free speech as something that only serves 'old white rich men'. That's how much of the left now views free speech—as a tool of the empowered, a con that allows pampered folks only to say what they think. With such a deeply cynical view of perhaps the most important political value, one which earlier leftists fought tooth-and-nail to defend, it is little wonder that the right can now claim supreme moral authority over freedom of speech—that authority has been ceded to it by a left that has ditched its old free-wheelin', state-suspicious beliefs in favour of seeking to control thought and speech in the name of protecting the environment, pacifying the public and maintaining social order; something the right was once obsessed with doing.

Brandis isn't defending racists, as his illiberal critics claim: he's defending the Enlightenment-era principle that the state shouldn't get to determine what people can think and say. As another bottle of wine arrives, he returns to Mill: 'He said the only limitation on the freedom of the individual should be when he causes harm to others. Hearing views that you find offensive or outrageous or insulting is not a form of harm. If it is admitted to be a form of harm, then freedom of speech, freedom of discourse, intellectual freedom and political freedom become impossible.'

spiked, 17 April 2014

5. Brandis postscript

In caving into censorious chattering-class pressure and ditching its plans to reform Section 18C, Tony Abbott's government has failed its own free-speech test.

George Brandis set the test when I met him at the political haunt of Machiavelli's in Sydney to interview him for my online mag *spiked*. Lubricated with wine, the liberty-loving words of Voltaire and John Stuart Mill fizzing in his mind and falling from his mouth, Brandis told me that standing up for the free-speech rights of the hateful and the horrible was the ultimate test of a nation's devotion to freedom. It's no good only defending freedom of speech for folks whose ideas chime with your own, he said—you must also 'defend the right of people to say things you would devote your political life to opposing. That's the test.'

He's right, it is. The measure of a man's commitment to liberty has long been whether he will do the decent Voltairean thing of defending to the death other people's right to think, utter, scribble and publish stuff that he himself finds foul. And it seems the Abbott government won't. The Abbott government will not, after all, defend freedom of speech for all, which ultimately means you don't have freedom of speech in Australia. You have state-approved speech—speech rights for those decreed by the government to be racially on-message, and therefore acceptable, but not for anyone else.

I don't buy the idea that the reason Abbott took the 'leadership call' to park the plans to overhaul Section 18C—which forbids insulting, humiliating or intimidating a person or group on the basis of their race or ethnicity—is because those plans had become a 'complicating' factor in his government's dealings with the Muslim community.

Apparently the PM was concerned that watering down Section 18C would weaken his ability to win the backing of Muslim groups for tough new terror laws, some of which are pretty authoritarian themselves. In short, he decided to keep a law that censors intellectual reprobates in the name of making it easier to pass a law that will empower the state to retain citizens' online data. What a double-whammy wallop to the face of liberty! In essence the PM is saying, 'We need to keep censorship in place in order to make it easier for us to introduce laws to spy on you', which is enough to make a liberal like me (and Brandis, surely?) sob into my dog-eared copy of *On Liberty*.

But I think there's more to the sellout on Section 18C than Muslims. The real problem is the distinct and depressing lack of appetite in modern Australia, and across the Western world today, for full-on, balls-out free speech.

The flak Brandis got simply for saying 'I think everyone should have freedom of speech' was remarkable. He was shrilly accused by the weirdly illiberal small-L liberals that make up modern Oz's chattering classes of unleashing bigotry, of endangering the lives of poor little ethnic people through giving a green light to the expression of crazy hateful nonsense. It spoke volumes about the modern left's Stalin-style allergy to liberty, their searing distrust of the gruff public, that they could so casually equate freedom of speech with violence, fantasising that the utterance of problematic ideas would instantly lead to real-world roughings-up and possibly pogroms. Like every other censor in history, from the Inquisition's warriors against heresy to the stuffy British judges who banned *Lady*

Chatterley's Lover, the pro-Section 18C mob was driven by the poisonous conviction that the little people are too volatile to be able to hear outré ideas and thus must have their eyes and ears covered by the cool-headed censors of officialdom.

Tragically, this illiberal creed, this belief that words cause mayhem because the public is stupid and suggestible, is deeply entrenched today. It informs debates on everything from climate change (if you deny this orthodoxy apparently the world will be plunged into eco-apocalypse) to so-called 'rape culture' (if blokes see saucy images of women they will become rapists, because they are basically robots). This modern fear of freedom, which is at root a fear of the rabble and what it might do if it reads outrageous words, makes it really hard to be a true Voltairean today. At a time when to be an out-and-proud fighter for free speech means you will be branded a facilitator of bigotry and apocalypse, it can sometimes feel preferable to say: 'Okay, you win, I'll add a "but" to my commitment to free speech.' Which is what the Abbott government has now done: 'We believe in freedom of speech, but not for racists…'

We need to recognise what a terrible impact such liberty-qualifying 'buts' have on the Enlightenment values of freedom and tolerance. Something like Section 18C, a massive 'but' to free speech, does two things: it strangles liberty through forbidding the expression of certain ideas, and, in a terrible irony, it makes it harder to challenge hatred and prejudice.

Section 18C polices thought and speech through allowing the state to dictate which ideas are acceptable, which not. This doesn't only impact on people who really do spread racist BS but also on those, like Andrew Bolt, who simply have un-PC political views on multiculturalism or immigration. That is, like every other act of crude, clumsy censorship in history, it punishes the politically non-conformist as well as the bovinely prejudiced. And 18C fails to stand up to hatred through helping to push hateful ideas underground. This is a massive problem with anti-hate speech laws: in silencing hateful opinion they deny to the rest of us, the right-minded majority, the right to have a reckoning with such ideas, to know them and wage war on them. They push hatred underground, where it festers, sweats, grows, unchallenged by free and open public ridicule. Don't believe me? Look at France. Twenty years ago it banned Holocaust denial, yet today it has a major anti-Semitism problem. The banning of Holocaust denial ironically made it seem more enticing to certain sections of French society, and they indulged in it in hidden forums, safe from the rational challenges of people who know their facts and don't hate Jews.

This is what we lose when something like 18C stays on the statute books: the freedom to speak our minds and the ability to tackle hatred. Abbott's about-face on Section 18C is a dark day for Australia.

The Spectator, 9 August 2014

6. STILL BRUCE

The *Vanity Fair* photo of Bruce Jenner in a boob-enhancing swimsuit is being described as iconic. Bruce, one-time American athlete, now wants to be known as Caitlyn, having recently undergone some gender transitioning. And he's using the cover of *Vanity Fair* to make his 'debut as a woman'. Next to the headline 'Call me Caitlyn', he's all photoshopped svelteness, pampered hair and look-at-me breasts, in what many experts are already calling 'an iconic image in magazine history'.

The photo is indeed iconic. And not just in the shallow celeb meaning of that word. It's iconic in the traditional sense, too, in that it's being venerated as an actual icon, a devotional image of an apparently holy human. It's an image we're all expected to bow down to, whose essential truth we must imbibe; an image you question or ridicule at your peril, with those who refuse to genuflect before it facing excommunication from polite society. Jennermania confirms how weirdly authoritarian, even idolatrous, trans politics has become.

There is a palpable religiosity to the wild hailing of Bruce/Caitlyn as a modern-day saint, a Virgin Mary with testicles. Within four hours of its launch, more than a million people were following Bruce/Caitlyn's Twitter account, hanging on his words like the expectant horde waiting for Moses at the foot of Mount Sinai. His every utterance, all banal celeb-speak, was retweeted tens of thousands of times. Celebs and commentators greeted Caitlyn as a kind of messiah. 'We've been waiting for you with open arms', said an overexcited editor at *Buzzfeed*. Across the Twittersphere

Caitlyn was worshipped as a 'goddess', a 'goddess in human form', a 'goddess made manifest on Earth'. 'Caitlyn Jenner could fucking stab me right now and leave me for dead and I'd die fucking overjoyed we are not WORTHY OF THIS GODDESS', said one trans tweeter, and she wasn't joking.

In the media, the talk is of how Caitlyn and her iconic likeness might give an adrenalin shot to humanity itself. A writer for the *Guardian* describes Caitlyn as a 'queen' and instructs us to 'bow down, bitches', telling us Caitlyn's icon on the front of *Vanity Fair* is 'life-affirming'. Treating Caitlyn as a kind of Christ figure, only in a push-up bra rather than smock, Ellen DeGeneres says this goddess brings 'hope for the world', and we should all try to be 'as brave as Caitlyn'. Susan Sarandon celebrated Bruce/Caitlyn's mysterious 'rebirth' while Demi Moore thanked him/her for sharing with humanity 'the gift of your beautiful authentic self'. A writer for the *Huff Post* says the name Caitlyn means 'pure'— 'what a perfect meaning, right?'. Truly, yes, for St Caitlyn, reborn to educate us all, is most pure.

With its millions of agog followers, its worship of an iconic image, its insistence we all 'bow down', the Cult of Caitlyn gives Catholic mariolatry a run for its money in the blind-devotion stakes. And of course, as with all venerated icons, anyone who refuses to recognise the truth of Caitlyn's *Vanity Fair* cover will face mob punishment or finger-wagging corrections of their goddess-defying blasphemy.

So when Drake Bell, a former American child star, tweeted 'Sorry… still calling you Bruce', he became the subject of global fury. The Cult of Caitlyn went insane. Even after Bell deleted his blasphemous comment, tweeters mauled him, suggesting he deactivate his Twitter account, or better still, 'deactivate his life'.

Meanwhile, a Twitter robot called @she_not_he has been set up to correct any 'misgendering' of Caitlyn. Winning high praise from much of the media, this bot is 'scrubbing Twitter, looking for anyone who uses the "he" pronoun in conjunction with Caitlyn Jenner's name'. The bot's inventor says he is delighted that these misgendering miscreants have been 'apologetic in their replies to the bot', and 'some have even deleted their original tweet'.

In short, they've repented. Just as those who denied the divinity of Christ were once expected to recant their heresy, so those who deny the gender of Caitlyn Jenner are hounded by bots into apologising for their moral error. The American gay-rights group GLAAD is scouring the mainstream media for any use of the word 'he' in relation to Caitlyn, like a modern incarnation of the Vatican's *Index Librorum Prohibitorum*, which monitored the public sphere for any less-than-gushing commentary on God. It has issued speech-policing guidelines for the media. 'DON'T refer to her by her former name… DO avoid using male pronouns and Caitlyn's prior name, even when referring to events in her past.'

The worship of Bruce/Caitlyn, and the hectoring of anyone who refuses to scrape before his/her icon, has graphically exposed the intolerant edge to trans thinking. The insistence that we not only refer to Bruce/Caitlyn as 'she' but also project this backwards—recognising, in the words of the *Guardian*, that she has 'always been a woman'—is borderline Orwellian. It's a rewriting of history, a memory-holing of old inconvenient facts. Strikingly, the *Guardian* writer says people like Bruce/Caitlyn have 'always been women… even when they were "fathering" children'. Notice it's the 'fathering' bit that is in scare quotes, suggesting it wasn't real, while the description of Bruce as a woman is treated as an incontestable truth. War is peace, freedom is slavery, man is woman.

This trans Orwellianism is increasingly finding expression in the law itself. In Ireland, a trans woman has won the right to have her sex changed to female on her actual birth certificate. This is alarming. The midwife who said 'This is a boy' when this trans woman was born was telling the truth, and that truth was recorded on a public document. No matter—truth and history are putty in the hands of the trans lobby. Just as Big Brother thinks it can force people to accept that $2 + 2 = 5$, so trans activists want us to chant: 'Bruce Jenner is a woman and has always been a woman, even when she was producing sperm, impregnating women, and winning gold medals in men's sports.' And the small matter of Bruce's birth certificate, his proven paternity of children, his *penis*? Forget all that; shove it down the memory hole.

What the Cult of Caitlyn confirms, beyond a doubt, is that there's nothing progressive in trans politics. It is shrill, censorious, unreal, demanding compliance, punishing dissent. Progressives should reject it. Jesus was not the Son of God, Bruce Jenner is not a woman, and, I'm sorry, but $2 + 2 = 4$, and it always will.

The Spectator, 2 June 2015

7. THE TROUBLE WITH GAY MARRIAGE

The most striking thing following the Irish referendum on gay marriage is how few people are talking about gay marriage. Amid the near-global cheering that greeted the vote in favour of instituting gay marriage, there was barely any commentary on the institution of gay marriage. Sure, there was a handful of on-air marriage proposals in Dublin as the news cameras rolled, and the tailend of a BBC TV report informed us when the first gay marriages in Ireland would take place (Autumn). But given that this referendum was all about opening up a social institution to which gays had apparently been brutally denied entry, the lack of post-referendum talk about actual marriage was remarkable.

Instead of saying 'We can finally get married', the most common response to the referendum result from both the leaders of the Yes campaign and their considerable army of supporters in the media and political classes has been: 'Gays have finally been validated.' Across the spectrum, from the drag queens who led the Yes lobby to the right-wing politicians who backed them, all the talk was of 'recognition', not marriage. Ireland's deputy PM Joan Burton said the Yes vote was about 'acceptance in your own country'. Writing in the *Irish Examiner*, a psychotherapist said 'the referendum was about more than marriage equality… it was about validation and full acceptance [of gay people]'. PM Enda Kenny also said the referendum was about more than marriage—it was a question of gay people's 'fragile and deeply personal hopes [being] realised'. Or in the words of novelist Joseph O'Connor, the Yes vote was an act of 'societal empathy' with a section of the population.

The official Yes campaign went so far as to describe the Yes victory as a boost for the health and wellbeing of all Irish citizens, especially gay ones. A spokesperson said 'the effect of legal equality goes beyond the letter of the law... it enters our daily lives and our interaction with others'. In 'embracing' gay people, Ireland had 'improv[ed] the health and wellbeing of all our citizens'. In short, the Yes result made people feel good. A writer for the *Irish Times* described his gay friends' pre-referendum 'nagging shadow', a 'feeling that [they are] less somehow', and he claimed the Yes victory finally confirmed for them that they now enjoy society's 'support, kindness and respect'. Fintan O'Toole said the Yes victory was about making gays feel 'fully acknowledged'.

And you thought it was about marriage? How wrong you were. All the commentary on how the referendum was 'about more than marriage', how it went 'beyond the letter of the law' to touch on something deeper, something psychic, confirms that the campaign for gay marriage is not about achieving social equality—no, it's about securing parity of esteem, which is very different. The march of gay marriage has a stronger relationship with the new culture of therapy, and the need for recognition, than it does with the more longstanding ideal of legal equality and the need for rights. What is being sought here is not really the right to marry but rather social and cultural validation of one's lifestyle—'societal empathy' —particularly from the state. What we have witnessed in Ireland is not a new dawn of social equality but the further entrenchment of the value of cultural equality, and this is far from positive.

Ireland's focus on recognition rather than rights, and the celebration of gay marriage as a means of validating gay people's sense of worth, echoes the discussion about gay marriage in nations across the West. Time and again, the language used has been that of therapy rather than autonomy. In her 2004 essay 'The liberal case against gay marriage', the American writer Susan M Shell noted the way that early agitators for gay marriage seemed to be primarily concerned with 'relieving adult anxiety', what some of them referred to as their 'elemental fear' of not being 'valued'. Activists spoke of how 'the lack of legal recognition [for our relationships] rankled more and more'. In the words of the authors of *The Politics of Same-Sex Marriage* (2007), activists primarily want 'the sanction of the state for our intimate relationships'. This search for state sanction, for external recognition, has been echoed in the response to the Irish referendum. 'My country has acknowledged that we exist', said a gay Irish businessman.

What we have here is not the politics of autonomy, but the politics of identity. Where the politics of autonomy was about ejecting the state from gay people's lives—whether it was Stonewall rioters kicking the cops out of their bars or Peter Tatchell demanding the dismantling of all laws forbidding homosexual acts—the politics of identity calls upon the state to intervene in gay people's lives, and offer them its recognition, its approval. For much of the past 50 years, radical gay-rights activism was in essence about saying 'We do not need the approval of the state to live how we choose'; now, in the explicit words of *The Politics of Same-Sex Marriage*, it's about seeking 'the sanction of the state for our intimate relationships'. The rise of gay marriage over the past 10 years speaks, profoundly, to the diminution of the culture of autonomy, and its replacement by a far more nervous, insecure cultural outlook that continually requires lifestyle validation from external bodies. And the state is only too happy to play this authoritative role of approver of lifestyles, as evidenced in Enda Kenny's patronising (yet widely celebrated) comment about Irish gays finally having their 'fragile and deeply personal hopes realised'.

What is being sought through gay marriage is not the securing of rights but the boosting of esteem. And this is a problem for those of us who believe in liberty. For where old, positive forms of social equality were a narrowly legal accomplishment, concerned simply with either removing discriminatory laws or passing legislation forbidding discrimination at work or in the public sphere, cultural equality is far more about ... well, culture; the general outlook; even people's attitudes. It is not satisfied simply with legislating against discrimination and then allowing people to get on with their lives; rather, it is concerned with reshaping the cultural climate, discussion, how people express themselves in relation to certain groups. In the apt words of the Yes campaign, this goes 'beyond the letter of the law'. It is undoubtedly the business of society to ensure social equality for gays, so that they may work and live as they choose free from persecution or harassment. But is it the job of society to ensure that there is parity of esteem for gays? That they feel good? That they feel validated, respected? I would say no, for then we invite the state not simply to remove the barriers to gay people's engagement in public life but to interfere at a much more psychic level in both gay people's lives, in order to offer 'sanction for their intimate relationships', and in other, usually religious people's lives, in order to monitor their refusal to validate gay people's lifestyles and offer them 'support, kindness and respect'.

This is why we have seen, across the West, the bizarre 'gay cake' phenomenon, where there are more and more cases of traditionalist bakers (and other businesses) being purposefully approached by campaigners to provide services to gay weddings. The aim of this very modern form of religious persecution is to discover and expose those whose attitudes have not yet been corrected by the top-down enforcement of parity of esteem for gays. That cultural equality is concerned not merely with altering laws, but with reshaping culture and even belief itself, is clear from the growing trend for harassing those who do not bow before the altar of gay marriage. Joan Burton made clear that this trend will now intensify in Ireland, when she said there will be no 'conscience clause' in the New Ireland: it would be intolerable, she said, to 'exclude some people or some institutions from the operation of marriage equality'. That is, all must agree, all must partake; there can be no room for the exercise of individual conscience when it comes to the engineering of a new cultural climate.

What Ireland crystallises is that gay marriage has nothing to do with liberty. The presentation of this as a liberal, or even libertarian, issue is highly disingenuous. For in truth, gay marriage massively expands the authority of the state in our everyday lives, in our most intimate relationships and even over our consciences. It simultaneously makes the state the sanctioner of acceptable intimate relationships, the ultimate provider of validation to our lifestyle choices, while empowering it to police the cultural attitudes and consciences of those of a more religious or old-fashioned persuasion. This is bad for gays, because it reduces them, in Kenny's words, to 'fragile' creatures who require constant recognition from others; and it is bad for those uncomfortable with gay marriage, since their ability to act in accordance with their conscience is limited. Making the state the validator of our intimacies and the policer of our moral outlooks is a very dangerous game.

This goes some way to explaining why every single wing of the Irish state supported gay marriage, from the police, who proudly waved the rainbow flag, to all the political parties, the public sector, the health establishment and the cultural establishment.

It's because they recognise, at a gut level, that unlike pretty much every other demand for liberty or equality in modern times, the campaign for gay marriage does nothing to threaten their authority—on the contrary, it expands it, in a way that the most authoritarian among them could only have dreamt of. Strikingly, Fintan O'Toole celebrated the referendum result by saying that 'Ireland has left tolerance far behind', by which he meant that the New Ireland actively encourages 'respect', not 'mere toleration', of minority groups. He's right, but not in the way he thinks: the new era of state-monitored cultural equality, of expanded state authority over more and more areas of our intimate lives and moral beliefs, does indeed mean that Ireland is leaving tolerance behind, and looks set to become a less tolerant country.

spiked, 27 May 2015

8. DON'T KILL YOURSELF

Is it wrong to commit suicide? A few years ago, society would have had little problem answering that question, and might have looked askew at you even for asking it. Of course it's wrong to commit suicide. It's nihilistic and destructive and damaging to individuals—most obviously to the suicide but also to the friends, family and community that his self-obliteration is fundamentally a blast against.

But today, society is far less sure about how to answer questions on the wrongness of suicide. It now goes something like this: 'Is it wrong to commit suicide? I don't know. Maybe. Maybe not. Let's not judge.'

The inability of our societies to adopt a clear moral stance on suicide was thrown into sharp relief by the suicide of Robin Williams. Williams' sad, untimely death exposed the extent to which we are now actively discouraged from criticising suicide. So when an American actor tweeted his belief that suicide is 'a very selfish act', in which an individual in turmoil is clearly 'not thinking about [his] family, [his] friends', he was subjected to worldwide Twitterfury and eventually had to recant and apologise for his anti-suicide sentiments. A Fox News anchor was likewise internationally harangued for describing suicide as 'cowardly'. Media outlets openly chastised criticism of suicide in the wake of Williams' death, with one long British newspaper article informing us that suicide is not a selfish act, and anyone who says it is could be doing 'more harm in the long run'. Suicides are 'NOT cowardly or selfish', decreed a headline in the UK *Daily Mirror* (its capitals).

The reprimanding of Robin Williams' critics echoes earlier controversies around the criticism of suicide. Following the suicide of Welsh football manager Gary Speed in 2011, the English footballer Joey Barton described suicide as 'one of the most tragic, most selfish, most terrible acts out there'—and he was branded 'sick' by the tabloids and self-styled experts for having done so. Frequent foot-in-mouth victim Jeremy Clarkson also found himself in the eye of a Twitterstorm when he described people who commit suicide on the London Underground as 'very selfish'. Meanwhile, the mental-health charity the Samaritans and others issue guidelines to the media about how to cover suicide, imploring hacks to report it in a super-sensitive, non-judgemental fashion.

The turnaround in society's attitude to suicide has been extraordinary. Once, it was those who considered or committed suicide who were described as 'sick'—now it's those who criticise suicide who are branded with the s-word. Once, suicide was treated as the ultimate taboo—now it's taboo to speak ill of suicide, to say it is bad or immoral or, as that Fox News anchor said of Robin Williams' suicide, 'horrible'. Where once all forms of suicide were pathologised, now casting moral judgement on suicide has become pathologised, being increasingly interpreted as a signifier of a swirling, warped mind. Yes, yesteryear's treatment of suicide as taboo, even as a crime until 1961 (in England and Wales), was problematic, not least because it had the consequence of discouraging the suicidal from seeking help. But the new treatment of criticism of suicide as taboo is also very bad, for it speaks to society's inability to uphold the value of life, the value of struggling to exist, and it could have the unwitting effect of turning suicide into something normal, possibly even positive.

What we're witnessing is the wrenching of suicide from the

sphere of moral judgement. Sure, society generally still believes that suicide is a sad event, and tries to tackle it. But it increasingly does so in a narrowly technical way. Some officials now treat suicide as something akin to school exam results, setting themselves targets for reducing the scale of the problem. 'Reduce the suicide rate between 2002 and 2013 by 20 per cent': that has been the Scottish government's target over the past decade, as if suicide were like road accidents—something that might be pretty straightforwardly reduced through a few technical interventions.

But of course, a suicide is not the same as a car crash. It raises infinitely more moral questions than an accident ever could: moral questions about the relationship between the individual and the community, about the social cohesion of society, about the value of life. To implement technical suicide-reduction strategies while simultaneously chastising any moral criticism of suicide is profoundly self-defeating, for without a moral position on suicide it is impossible truly to understand this act, far less send a signal about its wrongness and destructiveness.

But today, it's even worse than society simply refusing to judge suicide—increasingly, society implicitly celebrates suicide, treating it effectively as a legitimate lifestyle choice. That *Daily Mirror* article which in the wake of Robin Williams' death said suicide is 'NOT selfish' went even further—it described people who commit suicide in response to feelings of depression as 'incredibly brave' and 'unbelievably selfless'. In short, suicide can be a moral good. This view has received social and governmental sanction in recent years through the legalisation of assisted suicide—or the bizarrely named 'right to die'—in more and more Western nations. Today, not only does society refuse to judge suicide; it actually aids and abets it, providing to its citizens something which Aldous Huxley

only fantasised about in *Brave New World*: 'suicide buildings' in
which an individual who wants off this mortal coil is actively
assisted by officialdom.

In some European countries, one of the legitimate criterion
for being granted an assisted suicide is that you are 'tired of life'.
'Tired of life'—that sad phrase captures very well what is motoring
today's separation of suicide from moral judgement and the
creeping treatment of suicide as possibly good, possibly brave. It
is society-in-general's tiredness with life, its disillusionment with
humanity, which has led to the ringfencing of suicide from moral
criticism. Ours is an era in which humanity is seen as a burden, as
an ugly 'eco-footprint' on the planet, as a usurper of nature and
waster of resources; in which the birth of more babies leads to
doom-mongering about out-of-control population growth and in
which the medicine-assisted breakthrough of longer life leads to
handwringing about a 'silver tsunami' of grasping old people taking
up too much space and stuff. It isn't only some individuals who are
'tired of life'—society itself now frequently expresses a sense of
exhaustion with life, with humanity, with the human project itself,
and this has unquestionably contributed to the rehabilitation of
suicide as an understandable and possibly even legitimate act.

This is bad, because how society responds to a suicide is
incredibly important. It is no good having suicide-reduction
schemes or lists of words journalists covering suicide should avoid
using if at the same time you emit a subtle but distinctive signal
that says suicide is beyond moral critique. That can only help to
normalise suicide, to treat it as just another form of behaviour.
But it isn't just another form of behaviour. It's an act that ought to
feel devastating to us all, because it speaks to a profound rupture
between an individual and the community, between an individual

and us, even if we did not personally know him. In the words of the 20th-century writer GK Chesterton, 'The man who kills a man, kills a man. The man who kills himself kills all men, for as far as he is concerned he wipes out the world.'

As a humanist, I can understand why some individuals choose to end their lives, and I can empathise with deeply troubled individuals like Robin Williams. But as a humanist I also want to assert, as loudly as possible, the wrongness of suicide, to say that it is wicked and immoral and a betrayal of human values, to say that I am angry about what Williams did to himself and to the world. Suicide harms individuals and it harms society. Choose life.

spiked, 21 August 2014

9. MY PAINEITE HEART

There is something undeniably sad about the Thomas Paine Cottage in New Rochelle, New York. Fifteen miles outside of Manhattan, in a town that is half black youth, half preppy students (Iona College is here), the cottage where Paine once lived stands as one of the few permanent monuments to him in the United States.

He might have been the greatest radical in that age of epoch-exploding radicalism—the 18th century—whose 1776 pamphlet *Common Sense* inspired and energised the American Revolution. Yet one of only a handful of likenesses of Paine in the US, a country he helped to give birth to, is the 100-year-old waxwork dummy sitting forlornly at a desk in a corner of this cottage, looking for all the world like *Rising Damp*'s Rigsby in britches rather than an 18th-century firebrand. 'Let me just fix his hair', says John Wright, keeper of the cottage. 'The schoolkids are a bit rough with him.'

It breaks my Paineite heart. George Washington has an entire city named after him. Thomas Jefferson has a magnificent memorial and library in DC. John Adams has a statue in Boston and busts across America. Yet without Paine, a 37-year-old former corset-maker from eastern England when he landed in America in 1774, it is unlikely there would have been a successful revolution against British domination, or it would certainly have taken a different course. As a bust of Paine at a quiet, people-free crossroads outside the cottage reminds us, Joel Barlow, the 18th-century American diplomat and poet, said that 'Without the pen of Paine, Washington would have wielded his sword in vain'.

And what thanks does he get? An ageing dummy with bad hair. And a statue in New Jersey. We're still a long way from Napoleon's proposal—that 'a statue of gold should be erected to Paine in every city in the universe'.

It's almost as if Paine is treated as the crazy uncle of American history. The waxwork dummy certainly looks like a crazy uncle: wonky, wasted, tragic. Never officially accepted as one of the Founding Fathers, Paine is memorialised here in New Rochelle rather than in DC or Boston or the heart of NYC.

Cottage keeper Wright says the political elbowing aside of Paine started in his own lifetime. He lived in this cottage in New Rochelle towards the end of his life, before his death in 1809, on a farm given to him by the state of New York for his services to American liberty. 'His finances were a disaster', says Wright. Having donated his royalties from *Common Sense* to Washington's armies in the war for independence (and let's not forget that *Common Sense* sold 120,000 copies in its first three months of publication, in a country of only two million free citizens), and unable to secure a pension from the new American government, the ageing Paine was reduced to sponging meals off the locals. 'Here is a kettle from a nearby bar, which was used to make tea for Paine', says Wright. It's next to a stove that has a plaque saying: 'This stove was presented by Benjamin Franklin to Thomas Paine, hero of the revolution.' Paine was being kept warm by the charity of his former comrades in the fight for a republic.

Saddest of all, there's a framed letter on the wall that Paine wrote to officials in DC in the early 1800s enquiring why he had been denied the right to vote in New Rochelle. 'Respected friends …', it begins. Admittedly it was mainly Paine's fault he couldn't vote. Having been made a French citizen for his equally immense services to the French Revolution, and having later declared himself a 'world citizen' ('my country is the world, my religion is to do good'), no one was really sure where he had voting rights. Still, Paine was annoyed to be told he wasn't officially a US citizen, as well he might have been—he virtually invented the idea of American citizenship.

What's more he hated living in New Rochelle. 'Hated it', says Wright, as he peels wax off a table in the Paine living room. 'It was too quiet for him.' At every opportunity, despite being in his latter years, Paine would travel to Manhattan for a coffee ('or something stronger', says Wright) and argue about politics in various clubs and pubs. When he died at the age of 72 in 1809, there were seven people at his funeral in New Rochelle. '[It would] wound any sensible heart', said one of the attendees, 'to contemplate who it was, what man it was, that we were committing to an obscure grave on an open and disregarded bit of land'.

Paine's fate, his ending up as a naff waxwork at a table in a little-visited part of New York rather than as a statue of gold in DC, is about far more than bad luck or bad finances: it reveals something important about the nature of the United States itself.

Modern America's tortured relationship with Paine, its inability to count him as a Founding Father (in 1997 the History Channel caused quite the stir by including him in that select number), really expresses its inability fully to see through the American revolution, to realise what the historian Harvey J Kaye described as 'the promise of America' in his 2005 book *Thomas Paine and the Promise of America*. Paine makes modern American leaders uncomfortable because they recognise that without his clear-eyed radicalism, the United States might not have come into existence in the way that it did; and they also recognise, and are often responsible for the fact, that the content of his clear-eyed radicalism has not been genuinely realised: his belief, in Kaye's words, that the 'so-called lower orders, not just the high-born and propertied, had the capacity both to comprehend the world and to govern it'

It is impossible to overstate the enormity of Paine's contribution to modern world history. More than anything the story of Paine reveals the importance of ideas to the project of changing the world. In both America and France in the late 1700s, sections of the population were agitated by British rule and monarchism respectively. And it was as a result of Paine's injection of ideas, his inflammatory pamphleteering, that this anger became transformed into a war for independence in America and a revolution for a new kind of republic in France. Not for nothing is Paine described by Kaye as 'possibly the most influential writer in modern human history'.

Prior to the publication of Paine's *Common Sense* in America in January 1776, only around a third of the delegates to the Continental Congress, the political body of the American Revolution, supported separation from Britain. The rest wanted only for the 'mother country' to grant its American subjects more rights and to ease the tax burdens. As late as 1775, the year before *Common Sense* was published, George Washington was still toasting George III after dinners, and Thomas Jefferson said: 'There is not in the British Empire a man who more cordially loves a union with Great Britain than I do.'

Paine changed all that. This Englishman, not yet 40 and of no significant social standing, argued in *Common Sense* for the immediate and complete separation of America from Britain: 'Even the distance at which the Almighty hath placed England and America is a strong and natural proof that the authority of

one over the other was never the design of heaven.' Ridiculing
Britain's hereditary principle and imperfect democracy, Paine urged
Americans to 'make a true revolution of their various struggles',
and to create a single nation state with a government constituted
for 'respublica ... or the public good', in which there should be a
Bill of Rights and 'above all things, the free exercise of religion
according to the dictates of conscience'.

Americans read it in their thousands. A New Yorker wrote to
his local newspaper: 'This animated piece dispels, with irresistible
energy, the prejudice of the mind against the doctrine of
independence, and pours in upon it such an inundation of light and
truth as will produce an instantaneous and marvellous change in the
temper, in the views and feelings of an American.' Within months,
Jefferson made his Declaration of Independence, and Paine joined
Washington's armies against Britain as a kind of intellectual soldier,
writing a 13-volume series called *The American Crisis* in the bloody
era of 1776 and 1777. If *Common Sense* helped to give rise to the
desire for independence, *The American Crisis* sustained it in the
face-off with the 'mother country'. 'These are the times that try
men's souls', wrote Paine (as quoted by Obama in his inauguration
address in 2009).

Not content with having created an intellectual 'land-flood that
sweeps all before it' in America, as one of his readers put it, Paine
later went to France and stirred things up there too. His defence of
the French Revolution, *The Rights of Man*, published in 1791 (part
one) and 1792 (part two), was burnt by conservatives in Britain,
and devoured by radicals in France. Paine later co-authored the
French revolutionaries' Declaration of the Rights of Man and of
the Citizen and was elected to the French National Convention
(where he had to have his speeches read out by other people, on

account of the fact that he didn't speak French). It is testament, perhaps, to the more radical nature of the French Revolution that there *is* a gold statue of Paine in Paris, rather than just a badly dressed waxwork.

Paine's writings are imbued with a passion for unfettered democracy and liberty for the individual, with a faith in human agency and the exercise of individual autonomy. In his belief that ordinary people—or as he preferred, 'workingmen'—had the capacity and the wherewithal both to understand and govern the world around them, Paine, in Kaye's words, was building on traditions of radicalism to 'transform the very idea of politics and the political nation'. And his very peculiar place in American history, says Kaye, speaks to the ongoing contradiction between the 'promise' of America (liberty and representation for all) and the 'reality' (numerous checks on the democratic process and on freedom). The problem with Paine is that his writings energised and emboldened the American Revolution, but now exist as a permanent reminder of the failure to push through and deepen that revolution. And so he's left here, a dummy at a table in New Rochelle, the awkward uncle to the Founding Fathers.

spiked, 17 November 2010

10. Why porn thrives

Claire Perry, adviser to David Cameron on 'preventing the sexualisation and commercialisation of childhood', thinks society is drowning in porn. She's made waves with her campaign to stop British kids from encountering so much sauciness, whether it's bonking on the web or a grinding, barely-clad Rihanna on TV. But others, particularly observers of an anti-Tory bent, claim this talk of rampant sexualisation, or 'pornification', is nonsense. Children are not being warped by images of naked flesh or slutty song lyrics, they say, and the Conservative war on sexualisation is simply an attempt to 'traduce liberal values'.

Who's right? The panickers about pornification or the chilled-out critics calling for calm? Neither. There is without doubt a problem of 'sexualisation' today, with sex now omnipresent in popular culture, on TV, in film. You don't have to be a blue-rinsed prude to recognise that there's something off about seven-year-old girls sitting around eating Wotsits while watching Lady Gaga whip her backing singers with a bicycle chain. But this so-called 'pornification' of society doesn't spring from the underbelly of the internet, or from MTV, or from Rihanna's thongs, or any of the other things Perry and her backers are fretting about. It's a consequence of deeper social trends, and primarily of the denigration of intimacy and demonisation of romance, which have led inexorably to the fetishisation of sex.

Everyone, it seems, has an anecdote to demonstrate that we live in a 'pornified' world. Mine is hearing my eight-year-old niece sing the words 'I love it when you get up on me' (Rihanna) in the same casual way I might have sung 'Scooby Dooby Doo, where are you?' when I was eight. But this is the problem with the debate about sexualisation: its reliance on anecdote, and more strikingly its obsession with imagery. Listening to Perry and others fretting over 'hypersexualisation', you could be forgiven for thinking that British society and the attitudes of its inhabitants were directly shaped by media images, whether it's S&M-inspired pop or billboard bra ads. In truth, it's far more likely to be the other way around: that all this media imagery of sex reflects a longer-term shift in society's and individuals' attitudes towards sex.

Because they recognise there is a problem but can't fathom what it's all about, Perry and others end up pushing unconvincing 'media effects' theories. They claim sexualised imagery and advertising are poisoning people's minds and attitudes, particularly children's, and are even shaping how we relate to potential partners. Their cluelessness as to the origins or meaning of what they brand 'pornification' means they often sound a bit like conspiracy theorists. 'We're seeing an alien, warped view of sex normalised into our culture, ingrained by the invisible hand of the market', says MP Diane Abbott. 'Our daughters are being abused by a culture of porn', says one commentator, as if porn were a sentient force, seeking out young girls to despoil.

Campaigners' obsessive focus on imagery means they end up promoting image-busting—that is, censorious—solutions. So the government's 2011 Bailey Review into the sexualisation of childhood called for a strengthening of the 9pm TV watershed and for the 'music, retail and magazine industries' to stop producing so much sexual stuff. Perry wants to stop young people from accessing porn on the internet (good luck with that). The campaigners are aware they come across as prudishly censorious and furiously try to deny the charge. 'I am in no way the Mary Whitehouse of this', insists Perry. 'We don't all want to be Mary Whitehouse', says a columnist keen to clamp down on pornified things. These ladies protest too much: the end result of their campaigning is indeed likely to be strengthened watchdogs and more cautious culture-producers.

We end up with the worst of both worlds: a ban-happy climate alongside a continued failure to get to grips with, far less address, what the government calls sexualisation but I think we should call the fetishisation of sex. To discover the origins of this culture, our leaders ought to look closer to home rather than finger-wagging at Rihanna. For today's weird attitude towards and depiction of sex cannot be separated from the culture of fear and suspicion that now surrounds relationships of human intimacy and commitment—a culture that officialdom has done its fair share to spread. It is fundamentally this, the problematisation of intimacy and the corresponding crisis of romance, that has given rise to the treatment of sex as a fetishised category, a commodity almost, a displacement activity for relationships.

Ours is an era in which intimacy is deemed dangerous and commitment is pathologised. There's a powerful trend for depicting closeness and intense love as things that might damage you. Government campaigns targeted at teenagers claim intimacy is risky, full of pitfalls, where you might experience 'emotional violence' (whatever that is) or 'being made fun of'. A British government-funded website about relationships, aimed at young people, is called 'This Is Abuse', where everything from 'getting angry or jealous' to being 'called names'—all part and parcel of the most intimate bonds, surely?—is listed as a potential downside of getting close to another.

Meanwhile, the sinister-sounding phrase 'behind closed doors' is increasingly used to cast aspersions on intimate relationships between adults, including in marital homes. From the therapeutic world (where experts have discovered a new pathology: 'loving too much') to the policing sphere (where forces concentrate great effort on uncovering abusive relationships); from popular culture (where no one is ever happily married) to the publishing world (which churns out misery memoirs about raping dads and mad mums); from government circles (which obsess over domestic violence and rubbish parenting) to feminist activism (which treats the home as the most dangerous place on Earth, especially for women and children)—modern society's discomfort with intimacy is widespread, and suffocating.

These social shifts and moralistic campaigns have had a huge impact on how sex is viewed, discussed, and even experienced. This process was noted by Christopher Lasch in his seminal *Culture of Narcissism* (1979). He described how Western societies increasingly 'make a virtue of emotional disengagement' and how this can nurture 'a strict separation between sex and feeling'. In the modern period, 'intimacy is more elusive than ever', said Lasch; there's 'a revulsion against close emotional attachments', and this can lead to a 'desire to divest [sex] of the emotional intensity that unavoidably clings to it'. So sex becomes, not a way of achieving emotional closeness, but a means of avoiding it; perversely, we fuck in order to remain estranged.

This process has intensified in recent decades, giving rise to entirely fetishised forms of sex that are bereft of risky emotional entanglement or even feeling. At the most extreme end, we have the increased use of media for sexual gratification, whether by porn or through popular culture, which speaks to a desire to bypass human communication or interaction entirely in pursuit of sexual pleasure. But even in the more respectable realm of expert-led discussions about 'sexual health' or 'sexual wellbeing'—things we're all expected to cultivate these days—we can see the promotion of a fetishised form of sex that is focused far more on self-realisation than on engaging with, collapsing into, another human being. Sex is often pursued, not out of a longing for engagement with another, but as a means of avoiding precisely that. In such circumstances, it's inevitable that forms of culture have emerged which both reflect this relentless fetishisation of sex, and which also facilitate it, through the rise of web porn and 'porn identities' that provide for sexual activity without attachment. One of the great ironies of our times is that feminist campaigners spend a huge amount of time bemoaning pornification, yet they played a key role in facilitating it, through their problematisation of sex, intimacy, romance, the intensity of heterosexual commitment, and privacy ('the personal is political'), which interacted with other social trends in the late 20th century to encourage the emergence of new forms of intimacy-free, or intimacy-suspicious, sexual engagement. Porn being one.

The campaigners against sexualised imagery have got things upside down: it wasn't the images that changed the nature of sex and alienated us from one another; rather, the images speak to an already-existing, deeply rooted process of individual, social and sexual alienation. This is not to say that all sex must take place in a committed relationship, or be driven by love, that there isn't room for sleeping around. But when earlier generations experimented sexually, they were conscious of the fact that they were breaking boundaries: their sexual encounters could be measured, whether positively or negatively, against a broader cultural view of sex as an expression of deep feeling between two people. Today, there are no boundaries, no rules; there's only the collapse of what sex used to represent, and the corresponding rise of culture designed to get us off without ever having to submit ourselves to another. Porn thrives because romance has died, or rather has been bumped off, by the anti-intimacy anomie and profound fear-of-others so widespread in the 21st century. Tackling this slow, sad death of human emotional closeness and its replacement by a narcissistic cult of the self is, of course, far harder than telling Rihanna to put her bra back on.

spiked, 31 January 2013

11. RISE OF THE WANKERS

Masturbation used to be something everybody did but no one talked about. It was not most people's idea of a conversation starter. Certainly nobody boasted about being a self-abuser. It was seen as a sorry substitute for sex, a sad stand-in for intimacy.

Not any more. Masturbation has been reinvented as 'self-love', a healthy and positive form of self-exploration. Where once schoolboys were told it was a sin, now they're told it is essential to good health. A National Health Service leaflet distributed in schools advises teens to masturbate at least twice a week, because 'an orgasm a day' is good for cardiovascular health. The BBC is getting in on the act, too: its teen advice site insists masturbation is 'good for you as it helps relieve stress' and 'can help you sleep, and it may even help your genitals keep in top working order. It also allows you to explore what you enjoy.' And we wonder why so many teenage boys get hooked on internet porn.

Last month was International Masturbation Month, the brainchild of Good Vibrations, a purveyor of sex toys for singletons. Its aim? To spread the message that 'self-satisfaction is a healthy, accessible form of pleasure'. 'It's Masturbation Month! Give yourself a hand!' say the organisers. According to the Good Vibrations brigade, masturbation is just as good as having sex with someone else, and in some ways better. It is 'the safest form of sex a person can have'. Your hand is unlikely to give you an STD or break your heart, so it's preferable to intercourse with another living, breathing, unpredictable human being.

As part of International Masturbation Month, launched in

1995, there have been 'masturbate-a-thons' across the Western world. Individuals are sponsored to get to it, alone or in groups, to raise money for charity and to raise awareness about sexual health. The aim is to 'come for good causes'. Jesus wept. Britain's first such event took place in Clerkenwell in 2006, bringing together a bunch of pervs—sorry, awareness-raisers—who were sponsored for every minute they could pleasure themselves without … well, you know. It was supported by Marie Stopes International, Britain's leading abortion provider, which said the event was about 'dispelling the shame and taboos that persist around this most commonplace, natural and safe form of sexual activity'.

If you're too bashful to be a charity onanist, you can always sneak on to Amazon and buy any number of books dedicated to celebrating the subject. Recent titles include: *The Joy of Self-Pleasuring: Why Feel Guilty About Feeling Good?*; *Sex for One: The Joy of Self-Loving*; *Masturbation as a Means of Achieving Sexual Health*; and *The Big Book of Masturbation: From Angst to Zeal*.

All these tomes are devoted to stripping away the awkwardness and redefining the act as a legit form of sex, even an act of love. It speaks to the narcissism of our times that it's considered good to have a sexual relationship with oneself. Narcissus fell in love with his reflection; today young people are urged to fall for their own genitals.

The key conceit of today's celebrators of masturbation is that they are smashing taboos. They fancy themselves as free-spirited and open-minded, sticking one in the eye of sad, buttoned-up prigs. This gets things completely the wrong way round. The wanking evangelists are really enemies of free love: they're driven, deep down, by a fear of other people and a desire to dodge intimacy.

Betty Dodson, author of *Sex for One*, openly celebrates masturbation as preferable to the sometimes scary passion that accompa-
nies sex for two. The problem with romantic passion, she says, is
that 'reality comes crashing in, [and] the pain and the hurt and the
suffering and the breakdown follow'. The sanctification of self-
abuse is in keeping with today's general fear and distrust of Other
People, who will leave us hurt and damaged. The moral rehabilitation of masturbation is fuelled by anomie, an urge to withdraw
from the world, hardly a libertine impulse.

It was silly to tell children that masturbation was evil and would
make them blind or loopy. But it's sillier—and dangerous—to tell
youngsters that it is preferable to sex with others because it's risk-
free and passionless. We should keep the taboo that says that it
really is a bit sad. Hey kids, leave your bits alone—explore someone
else's.

The Spectator, 28 June 2014

12. COAL PRIDE

Why are so many Australians so sniffy about the coal industry? Everywhere I go I meet someone who has a beef with the black stuff. And it isn't just the usual suspects—those green-hearted weepers for Gaia who think any kind of rummaging in the earth for combustible resources is a crime against nature, and who are hilariously unaware that their unproductive lives of tweeting and thrift-shopping would be impossible if a couple of hundred years ago man hadn't burnt copious amounts of coal and in the process invented the modern world. No, even some Australians with brain cells are down on coal, talking about the scars it leaves in the Aussie earth and the black clouds of smog it raises over China. Uttering the word 'coal' can ruin a dinner party as surely as saying that other infamous four-letter c-word might have done a few years back.

I don't get this because, to my mind, Australia's coal industry is a wondrous, jaw-dropping thing. It should surely stir the heart that Australia unearths so much of this blackest of minerals, which has aeons-old sunlight trapped within it, and then exports it by the shipload to China and elsewhere, where the sunlight is unlocked and used to power progress and development. It should surely boggle the mind that 200,000 Aussies work in the coal industry, that they dig up a gazillion tonnes (or thereabouts) of coal a year, and that around 350 million tonnes of it is exported to nations that need and want this black rock's easily teased-out energy. Through its coal-digging antics, Oz has made itself the facilitator of numerous new industrial revolutions, the midwife of a new era of progress, the provider of energy to massive, bustling emerging cities that make even the great, coal-fuelled London of the 1800s look like a quaint village in comparison. We need some Coal Pride. Maybe even a Coal Pride bracelet. A black one, of course.

The knives are out for Australia's coal industry. The IPCC, the Vatican-like institution of permanent doom-mongering that issues scientific edicts with all the gusto that a medieval Pope would have churned out religious rules, recently said nations like Australia must stop exporting so much coal. Greenies were cock-a-hoop, because they've been arguing for yonks that Australia's spreading of the black stuff around Asia is basically a silent, creeping holocaust. *The Monthly* says Australia needs to 'keep its coal in the hole'. This is a country that is 'highly educated' and yet all it can 'figure out how to do [is] dig up black rocks and send them to China to burn', it says, with super snootiness. Exploiting Mother Earth's coal resources is 'un-Australian', says the un-Australian *Guardian*. Greenpeace chastises Oz for feeding China's 'insatiable appetite for coal', claiming China is 'coal-addicted'. From this perverse perspective, Australia is a kind of global drug dealer and China its desperate junky skank.

Just imagine if eco-miserabilists like this had been around during the first industrial revolution, if back then there had been an international body whose sole job was to finger-wag at the explorers for natural resources. Humanity would have been screwed. If moaning nature-lovers had successfully halted or even slowed down that revolution, the vast majority of us would still be serfs, slaving away on tiny patches of land for a rich man in a castle, never venturing further than our garden gates, and dying of TB or syphilis at the age of 32 without having ever read Shakespeare or heard Mozart.

Coal, you see—or, more accurately, man's discovery of its inner powers—was one of the great liberators of mankind. It was the fuel for a revolution that led to the building of cities, the creation of machines that could transport stuff to every corner of the globe, and the mass movement of men and women from the land into built-up places where within a few years they would demand the vote and education and other good things befitting their new city-dwelling status.

The war of words against China's current use of its own and Queensland's coal to motor a new industrial revolution is an attempt to prevent the East from undergoing the same technological, social and moral leap forward on the back of the black stuff that the West went through ages ago. By people whose very time-richness, whose ability to spend hours tweeting furiously about how horrible the coal industry is, is itself a by-product of the industrial revolution's creation of a whole new era of human productivity and leisure time. Charming.

I love coal. I find it endlessly fascinating. It has been essential to the expansion of human civilisation. Coal basically contains ancient sunlight; it stores the surging heat of the Carboniferous period, of about 300 million years ago, when our planet was so hot even I might have signed up to Greenpeace. About a thousand years ago, mankind started to liberate this trapped sunlight, burning coal to heat homes, which meant he was no longer reliant on forestland for wood and heat. Thus could more forestland be cut down, more cropland created and more foodstuffs made. Later came the industrial revolution, when coal's trapped sunlight was unleashed to motor trains, machines, factories and unprecedented movements of things and people. Man's discovery of coal, his unlocking of its hidden ancient energy, helped to make all the good stuff we currently enjoy—from cities to global travel to mass democracy—a reality.

And now Australia, by carving into the belly of its land and extracting its black guts, is helping other countries to bask in the benefits of this 300-million-year-old sunlight, too. Asia can't get enough of coal. China, which already accounts for half of the worldwide use of coal, plans to bump up its coal use by 14 per cent by 2020, with the help of Oz. India has doubled its coal use over the past 10 years. It's expected that coal use in the Asean nations will triple by 2035. And the benefits of all this coal-burning are enough to bring a tear to a proper progressive's eye. In China over the past 20 years, 250 million people, a vast swathe of humanity, have been lifted out of poverty. That wouldn't have happened without economic growth, which wouldn't have happened without coal, which Australia helps to provide.

Let's get our priorities straight. Right now, there are some things more important than tackling climate change, and one of them is delivering economic growth, energy, heat and light to the still-dark, still-poor bits of the world. Australian coal is doing its part in this great drive to industrialise more of the Earth, so be proud. Wear a black bracelet.

The Spectator, 26 April 2014

13. EARTH IS NOT FINITE

There's one eco-orthodoxy we really need to challenge: the idea that natural resources are finite; that we live on a finite planet and therefore we can only have a certain number of people, living in a certain number of homes, eating a certain amount of food. Nothing better illuminates the historical illiteracy and social pessimism of eco-panickers and modern-day Malthusians than their worry about stuff running out.

Malthusians are plain wrong to say natural resources are fixed and we can predict when they'll dry up. I know it seems commonsensical to say Earth is finite, and a bit mad to say it isn't. But it's important to recognise how fluid and changeable resources are. The usefulness and longevity of a resource is determined as much by us, by the level of social development we've reached, as it is by the existence of the resource in the first place. Natural resources are not fixed in any meaningful sense; what we consider to be a resource changes as society changes.

So in Ancient Rome, one of the main uses of coal was to make jewellery. Women liked the look of this glinting black rock hanging round their necks. No one could have imagined that thousands of years later, coal would be used to power massive steam engines and an entire industrial revolution, changing forever how we make things, and how we live.

Two thousand years ago, one of the few uses of uranium was to make glass look yellow. It was used to decorate windows and mirrors. You'd probably have been locked up, or subjected to an exorcism, if you had suggested that one day this window paint might be used to light up and heat entire cities, or destroy them.

The same resource can do very different things depending on our social and technological development. It was social limits, not natural limits, that meant Ancient Romans could not use coal to make things move, and other ancient communities could only use uranium to tint glass. The main problem with the resource-pessimists and population-growth hysterics of the green movement is that they continually misinterpret social limits as physical limits. They naturalise social limits, presenting problems of social development as problems of nature's shrinking bounty. They make the fatal flaw of believing that our ability to progress is determined by what nature has to give us, when in truth it is us, and our understanding of nature's secrets, who determine how far we can go.

This is why they're wrong about absolutely everything, why every prediction Malthusians have made has failed to materialise. A very early resource panicker, the second-century Christian philosopher Tertullian, said: 'We are burdensome to the world, the resources are scarcely adequate for us… already nature does not sustain us.' There were only 180 million human beings on the planet back then—about the same number that currently lives in the eastern part of the United States. The problem for Tertullian was his understandably limited imagination. In his time, pretty much the only known resources were animals, plants and various metals and minerals. Tertullian had no way of conceiving of the enormous abundance of resources inside the Earth, which lay dormant because of humanity's social and technological limits, not natural ones.

Thomas Malthus, the messiah of Malthusianism, argued in the late 1700s / early 1800s that food production wouldn't be able to keep pace with human reproduction, and as a result there would be 'epidemics, pestilence and plagues' that would bump off millions. Yet in his era, there were only 980 million people; today there are more than that in China alone, and they all have food to eat. Malthus's pessimism made him think it was impossible for mankind to develop beyond a certain, nature-determined point. And yet, shortly after he made his scary population pronouncements, through the industrial revolution, mankind overcame many of his limits and found new ways to make food and things and deliver them across the globe.

Population-panicking greens pose as a science-based movement that has worked out through equations and pie charts what the carrying capacity of the Earth is. But actually they make a schoolboy scientific error: to imagine that population is the only variable, the only thing that grows and grows, while everything else—resources, society, progress, discovery—stays roughly the same. Yet history shows that population is far from the only variable. Resources are a variable, too. So is mankind's vision and our ability to rethink and tackle problems. These things change and grow just as population does. Malthusian mathematics doesn't add up, because their social pessimism means they fail to factor in the most decisive variable of all: mankind's ingenuity.

Today, still, the main problem we face is social rather than natural. We live under a cult of sustainability, a social and political framework that says we shouldn't tamper too much with nature or the status quo. The cult of sustainability is anti-exploration, anti-experimentation, anti-risk: all qualities we'll need if we are going to make the kind of breakthroughs earlier generations made with coal, uranium and other natural stuff.

Malthusians' focus on finiteness doesn't only make them wrong — it also makes them misanthropes. Eco-worriers look at people as merely the users-up of scarce resources. They view nature as the producer of things and mankind as the consumer of things. Their finiteness obsession means they conceive of humanity as a kind of bovine force, hoovering up everything it comes across. In their eyes, humans are the cause of every modern ill, and thus reducing human numbers is the solution to every modern ill.

Eco-miserabilists see mankind as despoiler. They refer to our building of cities and factories as an 'eco-footprint', as if it's something dirty and destructive. Our use of natural resources such as wood and oil is referred to as the 'rape of the planet'. Even our use of water is now problematised, with charities telling us to measure our 'water footprint' and only shower every other day. We're encouraged to be 'water neutral'. In the past there was another word for 'water neutrality': death. No living thing known to man can survive without water, yet today we're supposed to feel guilty about using it.

This view of mankind as gorging on nature's fragile resources is not based on any hard scientific proof of widespread resource depletion. That's clear from the fact that even water is now included in the list of resources we should use sparingly: only a loon could believe water will ever run out. No, this view is based on a profound philosophical shift in our attitudes towards ourselves, a move from viewing humanity as tamer of the planet and creator of society, towards viewing him as a plague, a pox on Gaia.

It's a spectacularly one-sided view of people. Because we don't only use resources—we also create them. We're not only consumers—we're also producers. In fact, we have helped this planet to realise its potential. Without us it would just be another ball spinning through space stuffed with useless coal and pointless uranium. We extracted that coal and uranium and made something amazing with it: modern human society. We created the social conditions in which the Earth's resources could be used to their full potential; we created cities, workplaces and homes on the back of those resources. We haven't diseased the Earth; we've humanised it, improved it, turned it from something wild and violent into a liveable place for seven billion human beings. The 'human footprint' should be celebrated, not cleaned up.

Malthusians' view of mankind sometimes crosses the line from disdainful into something darker. A British 'population awareness' charity—what population controllers call themselves these days— recently launched a website called PopOffsets. It allows well-off Westerners to offset their carbon emissions by paying for people in the Third World to stop procreating. You log on, enter information about a flight you recently took or how much you've been driving your car, and then the site tells you how much carbon you have used and therefore how much you should donate to a Third World reproductive charity. That charity makes up for your carbon-use by cutting back on the pitter-patter of tiny carbon footprints in countries like Kenya. So if you took a round-trip from London to Sydney, that adds up to 10 tonnes of carbon, in which case you are asked to donate £40 to help prevent the birth of one African child.

This is the repulsive logical conclusion to the anti-humanism of our eco-era: wealthy Malthusian Westerners using African life as a bargaining chip in their mission to absolve themselves of eco-guilt. 'Taken a carbon-spouting holiday to Florida? Quick, prevent the birth of four grasping negros to make up for it!' The misanthropic penance of the rich Malthusian set.

Such misanthropy is a direct result of the fetish of finiteness. Because when you view human beings as the ravenous users of running-out resources, then you start to see human life itself as a pollutant, a drain on the planet. That is why Malthusians refer to every newborn child as 'another mouth to feed'. But human beings are not just mouths to feed—they're also brains that can think, minds that can create, hands that can work. They don't only need resources; they find and make them too.

Earth is not finite. The potential of this huge, resource-rich, wet planet is infinite. But in order to realise it fully, even more than we have already, we need to defeat the eco-Malthusianism that has become so mainstream, in order that we might use natural resources in new ways that earlier generations, even our own generation, never thought possible.

Speech in London, 30 October 2010

14. Dissent as disease

A few days ago, for a joke, I set up a Facebook group called 'Climate change denial is a mental disorder'. It's a satirical campaigning hub for people who think climate-change denial should be recognised as a mental illness by the American Psychiatric Association, and its sufferers offered 'eco-lobotomies' to remove 'the denying part of their brain'. The group now has 42 members. Yeah, some have signed up because they get the joke. But others are serious subscribers to the denial-as-insanity idea. 'Thank God I've found this group', says one.

The idea that so-called climate-change denial is a psychological disorder—the product of a kind of neural inability to face up to the catastrophe of global warming—is becoming more popular among green-leaning activists and academics. And nothing better sums up their elitism than this psychologisation of dissent. The labelling of any criticism of the politics of global warming, first as 'denial', and now as evidence of mass psychological instability, is an attempt to write off all critics as deranged, and to lay the ground for inevitable authoritarian solutions to climate change.

The University of West England recently hosted a major conference on climate-change denial. Strikingly, it was organised by the university's Centre for Psycho-Social Studies. It was a gathering of those from the top of society—'psychotherapists, social researchers, climate-change activists, eco-psychologists'—to analyse those at the bottom of society, as if we were so many irrational amoeba under an eco-microscope. The conference explored how 'denial' is a product of both 'addiction and consumption' and is the 'consequence of living in a perverse culture which encourages collusion, complacency and irresponsibility'.

Leading green writers welcomed the West England get-together to study the denying masses. Leo Hickman hoped the conference would generate ideas for dealing with those who are 'pathologically' opposed to the environmental movement. Pathology, according to my *OED*, is the study of 'morbid or abnormal mental or moral conditions'. Confirming the inherent elitism of environmentalism, Hickman said that where 'mainstream politics now largely "gets" environmentalism', there's still a sceptical mass, 'a baying and growing crowd, largely consisting of people resistant to the prospect of ever having to alter their lifestyles'. Apparently this crowd 'gathers to hurl invective' at environmentalist ideas.

In a sense, this vision of brainy environmentalists on one side and an insult-hurling crowd on the other speaks, however unwittingly and crudely, to an underlying truth: environmentalism remains an elitist project, beloved of politicians, priests and prudes keen to curb the public's excessive lifestyles, and it rubs many 'ordinary people' up the wrong way. Of course much of the public goes along with the environmentalist ethos, bowing to the central idea that mankind is destructive and observing such rituals as sorting their rubbish. But they do so half-heartedly, recognising that, fundamentally, greens' anti-consumerist, anti-reproduction, anti-travel arguments run counter to their own aspirations. Yet rather than recognise this frequently hidden divide between the green elite and the 'baying crowd' as one built on differences of opinion and interest, greens pathologise it, turning it into evidence of their wisdom in contrast to the public's mental instability.

University departments, authors, think-tanks and activists have embraced the 'psychological disorder' view of climate-change scepticism. At Columbia University in New York, the Global Roundtable on Public Attitudes to Climate Change studies the 'completely baffling' response of the public to the threat of climate change. Apparently, our slack response is partly a result of our brain's inability to assess 'pallid statistical information' in the face of fear. *The Ecologist* magazine focuses on the 'psychology of climate-change denial' and says the majority of people (excluding those 'handfuls of people who have already decided to stop being passive bystanders': the green elite) have responded to warnings of global warming by sinking into 'self-deception and mass denial'. An online magazine called *Climate Change Denial* is dedicated to analysing the public's 'disturbed' response to climate change.

John Naish, author of the anti-consumerism treatise *Enough!*, says the public's consumerist behaviour, with its promise of 'ecological disaster', ultimately springs from the fact we're using the 'wrong brain'. Our culture, all those flashy ads and temptations to buy, buy, buy, is aimed at stimulating our 'primordial instinct', our 'reptilian brain, which is responsible for arousal, basic life functions and sex', says Naish. It neglects and makes lazy our 'neocortex, the intelligent brain we evolved in the Pleistocene era'. In short, we're behaving like animals rather than intelligent beings. Indeed, Naish says our consumer culture is sending us '*knuckle-dragging* into ecological disaster'.

The labelling of those who question certain scientific ideas or green ways of life as 'deniers', 'addicts' and 'reptiles' has a deeply censorious bent. If climate-change questioning is a form of mass denial, a psychological disorder, then there's no need to engage with it meaningfully; instead people just need to be treated. Thus *The Ecologist* says 'denial cannot simply be countered with information'; indeed there is apparently 'plentiful historical evidence that increased information may even intensify denial'. A British think-tank, the Institute for Public Policy Research, goes so far as to insist that 'the task of climate-change agencies is not to persuade by rational argument but in effect to develop and nurture a new "common sense"'. This is the logical conclusion to treating dissent as a disorder: no debate, no real information, just an insidious demand to change The Culture in order to relax the wrong side of people's brains and inject us with a readymade 'commonsensical' outlook—that is, The Truth, as decreed by those who 'get environmentalism'.

The psychologisation of climate-change scepticism reveals how utterly cut off are eco-elitists from mass society. They cannot comprehend our behaviour, our thoughts, our desire to have families, our dreams of being wealthier, more comfortable, better travelled. For them, such behaviour runs counter to the 'extraordinary information' provided by scientists apparently showing that our lust for stuff will spell planetary disaster. They seriously expect people to make life decisions on the basis of pie charts and graphs drawn up in labs in Switzerland, rather than on the basis of what they and their families need and want. That the green lobby is so perturbed by our failure to act in accordance with scientific findings shows the extent to which, for them, The Science is a new gospel truth, and anyone who disobeys it a moral leper.

Psychologising dissent is the hallmark of authoritarian regimes. In the Soviet Union, outspoken critics of the party were frequently tagged as mentally disordered and faced, as one Soviet dissident described it, 'political exile to mental institutions'. In George Orwell's *Nineteen Eighty-Four*, O'Brien, the torturer in Room 101, offers to cure Winston Smith of his anti-party thinking.

'You are mentally deranged!' he tells him. Today it's greens who treat dissent as a disease and who long to come up with mental treatments for it. But questioning eco-orthodoxies is not madness; it's essential. It is the height of rational thinking, in fact, to challenge the backward notion that sinful mankind is destroying the Earth and that only self-imposed eco-penury and the stifling of criticism can save us.

spiked, 4 March 2009

15. Liberal racists

There are many mad and worrying things about the speech codes spreading across Western campuses like a contagious brain funk. There's their treatment of even everyday words as 'problematic' terms of abuse (one American university advises against referring to Arabs as Arabs). There's the branding of the most anodyne forms of friendly banter as 'aggressive' (according to the University of Wisconsin it is a 'microaggression' to say to a Latino or Native American, 'Why are you so quiet? We want to know what you think.') And there's the idea that even static objects can commit acts of violence against students: one university bemoans 'environmental microaggressions', which can include a college in which all the buildings are 'named after white heterosexual upper class males'. Even crossing the quad is a dangerous activity for today's fragile students. What these codes add up to is a demand that everyone be permanently on edge, constantly reevaluating their every thought before uttering it. It's an invitation to social paralysis.

But perhaps the worst thing about these tongue-clamping rules is how they incite hyper racial-consciousness. Indeed, some American college speech codes chastise students who *refuse* to think racially, who balk at the idea that they should always be actively mindful of their own and everyone else's racial make-up.

The 'problematisation' of students who refuse to think and behave racially is best captured in a University of California, Los Angeles (UCLA) guide to 'Recognising Microaggressions'. In keeping with other campus speech codes, the guide treats as dicey everything from simple questions (such as asking someone 'Where were you born?') to expressions of faith in meritocracy (like saying

'America is the land of opportunity'). But even more perniciously, it warns students and faculty members against being non-racial, telling them they must always 'acknowledge' other people's race.

UCLA says 'Colour Blindness', the idea we shouldn't obsess over people's race, is a microaggression. If you refuse to treat an individual as a 'racial/cultural being', then you're being aggressive. This is a profound perversion of what has been considered the reasoned, liberal approach for decades—that treating people as 'racial/cultural beings' is wrong and dehumanising.

UCLA offers the following examples as 'colour-blind' utterances that count as microaggressions:

'When I look at you, I don't see colour.'

'There is only one race: the human race.'

'I don't believe in race.'

Apparently such comments deny individuals' 'racial and ethnic experience'. But on a campus like UCLA a few decades ago, refusing to treat individuals as 'cultural beings' would have been the right and good thing. Now, in an eye-swivelling reversal, the opposite is the case: to demonstrate your politically correct virtue you must acknowledge the skin colour of everyone you meet.

The University of Wisconsin-Stevens Point similarly advises that colour-blindness is a racial microaggression. It lists 'America is a melting pot' as an aggressive phrase. It brands as problematic any comment by a white person that suggests he or she 'does not want to acknowledge race'. Anyone who claims to be 'immune to races'—that is, who prefers not to think about people as racial beings—is viewed as aggressive.

At the University of Missouri, the guide to 'inclusive terminology' lists colour-blindness as a form of prejudice, even as it recognises that this term 'originated from civil-rights legislation'. Once, colour-blindness was considered cool, but now we know it can be 'disempowering for people whose racial identity is an important part of who they are', says the school.

And in the University of New Hampshire's barmy guide to 'bias-free language', students are expected to take account of a person's skin colour, age and heritage before engaging with them. Whether they're being told that using 'American' to refer to people born in the US is wrong, or that they should call Arabs 'Western Asians' (what?), the message to students is clear: judge your acquaintance's skin colour, consider his or her cultural origins, and then decide what to say. Think racially, always.

Gwendolyn RY Miller, a diversity consultant who advises educational institutions on how to tackle racial microaggressions, says being colour-blind is a 'microinvalidation', since it serves to 'exclude, negate, or nullify the psychological thoughts, feelings, or experiential reality of certain groups'. She says the phrase 'We all bleed red when we're cut' is a microaggression. Perhaps Shakespeare was being microaggressive to Jews (and others) when he wrote his great, humanistic line: 'If you prick us, do we not bleed?' Miller says the claim that 'character, not colour, is what counts to me' is a racial microaggression too.

If that line sounds familiar, that's because it is almost exactly what Martin Luther King said in his 'I have a dream' speech. But American colleges in the 21st century demonise those who follow the King approach of judging people by 'the content of their character' rather than by the colour of their skin. Today, MLK would be viewed as naive at best and suspect at worst, conspiring to deny the primacy of our selves as 'racial/cultural beings'.

But here's the thing: King—like many other postwar radicals, liberals, and progressives—was challenging the idea that people should be engaged with and judged as 'racial/cultural beings'. He, and others, preferred to treat people as people, not as products or expressions of 'culture'. Now, 50 years on, the regressive, racial politics of identity has won out over that old humanistic dream of a post-race society, to such an extent that anyone who refuses to think of whites and blacks as different is treated as problematic.

New college speech codes don't only infantilise students and stymie open, frank discussion. They also point to the creeping re-racialisation of society, and to the rebranding of universalism itself as a form of racism. One of the great tragedies of the 20th century was that the demise of the old aggressive biological politics of race, cleaved to by many Western elites, did not lead to the creation of a post-racial world—on the contrary, the old racism was superseded by different forms of racialised thinking, in the guise first of a new race-relations industry and then of the politics of racial identity, which incites constant, myopic racial thinking. So entrenched is the new racial identitarianism that anyone who seeks to wriggle free from it, who bristles at the shoving of blacks and whites back into biological/cultural boxes, is treated as a pariah, as 'microaggressive'. To be truly anti-racist is a risky business today, thanks to the re-racialisation of everyday life by supposed liberals and the new identity set. Well, call me microaggressive all you like but, as a humanist, I refuse to treat my fellow citizens as 'racial/cultural beings'.

Reason, 5 August 2015

16. AGAINST CHOMSKY

Who sneeringly refers to the masses as a 'bewildered herd' and to sports fans as 'irrational jingoists'? Who argues that 'Joe Six Pack'—your average beer-swilling bloke—has been so battered by the mass media that it has 'reduced [his] capacity to think'? Prince Charles, perhaps, or some other posho who has no time or respect for *hoi polloi*?

Actually it's Noam Chomsky. The chattering classes' favourite radical believes the mass of the population can be made to think what the overlords of the mass media want them to think. And it is fundamentally this belief that endears him to laptop Leninists around the world. Chomsky adds a veneer of radicalism to these people's prejudices about the fickleness of the little people.

Chomsky wins high praise from the liberal elite. He's received the Sydney Peace Prize. He was voted the world's top public intellectual in a 2005 poll. Yet he is not the most startlingly original thinker. Much of his analysis rehashes the outlook of old patrician thinkers, doubters of the masses. Chomsky's chief contribution to contemporary political discourse has been to add a bit of spit and polish to elitist ideas, making them appear daring and radical.

His main focus is the power of the mass media and the way it 'dulls people's brains'. In his books *Necessary Illusions: Thought Control in Democratic Societies* and *Manufacturing Consent: The Political Economy of the Mass Media*, he pushed the idea that the media in Western democracies is no freer than it was in the Stalinist regimes of Eastern Europe. Because Western media outlets are generally corporate-owned, they are slaves to the free market, he argues, forever elevating business interests over the public interest. Let's leave aside the inconvenient fact that you cannot open a newspaper these days without seeing an editorial thundering against the evils and excesses of the free market. More pointedly, in order to believe, as Chomsky does, that the mass media is capable of 'brainwashing' Joe Six Pack and other undereducated inhabitants of mass society, you need to believe not only in the power of the media but also in the empty-headedness of the public.

The titles of Chomsky's books are revealing, with their warnings of 'thought control' and the 'manufacture of consent', as if the public's political beliefs, our very thought patterns, are easily controlled by external forces. Warming to this theme, Chomsky has referred to the '80 per cent of the population whose main function is to follow orders and not think'. Apparently, this swarm of people is mind-controlled either through the 'propaganda model', where the media tell them what to think about important issues, or through 'diversion', where the media divert people from thinking about important issues.

So Chomsky notes that much of this 80 per cent of the public are made to 'follow orders' and 'not think' through such things as competitive sports. Describing sport as a 'crucial example of the indoctrination system', he says it is promoted by the media as a way of 'building up irrational attitudes of submission to authority and group cohesion behind leadership'. Media outlets focus so much on sport because it is a form of 'training in irrational jingoism'; it's a way of reducing people's 'capacity to think'.

In short, the reason we go wild for Man United or our favourite Aussie rules team is because, unbeknownst to us, we have been conditioned by the media to ignore the big issues of the day and to become sport-crazed, subservient jingoists instead.

Chomsky frequently criticises the *New York Times* and the *Washington Post*, claiming these bastions of liberal thought are also part of the 'indoctrination system'. Yet he reserves his most snobbish ire for people who read trashy magazines, 'whatever you pick up on the supermarket stands'. They apparently spend their lives fretting over idiotic tabloid stories or reading astrology. Behind Chomsky's radical reputation, there lurks a snob.

This isn't surprising when you consider that much of his theorising on the moulding of public opinion borrows a great deal from aloof 20th-century intellectuals. Chomksy frequently cites Walter Lippmann, the American thinker who wrote a lot about the fickleness of public opinion. Indeed, the title of Chomsky's book *Manufacturing Consent* comes from a Lippmann line, from his 1922 book *Public Opinion*. Chomsky has even favourably cited Lippmann's view of the American public as a 'bewildered herd'.

Lippmann was one of the key anti-masses thinkers of the early 20th century. Much of the electorate is 'absolutely illiterate', he argued; in fact they are 'mentally children or barbarians' and therefore easy prey for 'manipulators'. Lippmann believed that only a better-educated class—those who 'saw clearly, thought rationally, acted disinterestedly'—could work out what was in the dumb public's best interests.

Today, in radical-sounding lingo, Chomsky and his army of admirers in Western liberal circles are resuscitating this idea. They might not be as explicitly disdainful as Lippmann was—preferring to describe the public as 'victims of thought control' rather than as 'barbarians'—but the underlying idea is the same: the masses are easily manipulated and thus we need an elite caste of thinkers to put them on the right road. It is striking that just as Lippmann clearly considered himself immune to the charms of 'manipulators', so

Chomsky and Co see themselves as immune to the mind control of the mass media and therefore morally superior to Joe Six Pack and the rest of the 'irrational jingoists' who read supermarket mags.

The alleged manipulability of the newspaper-reading blob has become the No1 source of handwringing among today's leftish elites. Ours is an era in which the people, and by extension the idea of democracy, is casually sneered at. From books like Bryan Kaplan's *The Myth of the Rational Voter*, praised by the *New York Times* for exposing that 'ordinary people' are 'lousy at recognising their own self-interest', to the fretting over the Murdoch Empire's newspapers and how they mould the little people into brainless racists and misogynists who obediently vote Liberal / Tory, the idea that individuals' thoughts can be manufactured by powerful actors is gaining strength.

Only today, this idea is most powerful on the left. In the past, as documented by John Carey in his book *The Intellectuals and the Masses*, it tended to be those of a very right-wing or aristocratically aloof persuasion who viewed the mob as fodder for media manipulation. As Carey says, early 20th-century European elitists viewed the masses as 'semi-human swarms, drugged by popular newspapers'.

Today, it's left-leaning patricians who do most to promote this view. They might have ditched the 'semi-human' talk, but they've clung to that old notion that people are drugged and dumbed down and made politically unhinged by the press and media. This media-effects theory—dumb person opens newspaper and is instantly turned into a jingoistic liability—speaks to the modern left's favourite idea, 'false consciousness': the notion that whereas we can think clearly and rationally—about war, poverty, the evils of capitalism—they, The Other, have had their consciousness colonised by popular media outlets and their evil mogul owners. The 'false consciousness' ideology adds a veneer of pretend-edgy, Frankfurt School-derived respectability to the old, more honest arguments of conservatives like Lippmann, who likewise believed there was a gaping divide between those who 'saw clearly, thought rationally' (Us) and those who were being manipulated (Them).

The new media-blaming has become the left's go-to explanation for its own demise, its failure to connect with the public. 'It's not our fault—it's because those people have been drugged by the press!' And thus does the left rehabilitate, in pseudo-progressive language, the paternalism of the old right. And Chomsky is their idol, today's main left reinvigorator of ugly old ideas.

The Australian, 5 November 2011

17. KANT VS THE KORAN

Following the unmasking of Jihadi John as Mohammed Emwazi, a London-raised computer-studies graduate of the University of Westminster, there's been a lot of media heat over the problem of campus radicalism. How did universities become breeding grounds for beheaders, ask startled observers, allegedly turning students into aspiring martyrs dreaming of spilling infidel blood and getting it on with 72 virgins? Universities are supposed to enlighten youngsters, not turn them into medieval decapitators. The Uni-panickers, including David Cameron, are now suggesting we should ban from campuses so-called hate preachers, those pontificating dispensers of Islamist dimwittery, in order to prevent impressionable minds from being twisted beyond repair.

But amid all this heat, there's also been a moment of light. It came in a *Washington Post* piece by Avinash Tharoor, who studied international relations at Westminster, Jihadi John's alma mater. Tharoor describes a seminar discussion of Kant's democratic peace theory in which something shocking happened. A student in a niqab scoffed at Kant and said: 'As a Muslim, I don't believe in democracy.' Even more shocking was the response. 'Our instructor seemed astonished but did not question the basis of her argument', says Tharoor. 'Why hadn't the instructor challenged her?', he asks, perplexed, especially considering that her Kant-bashing views, her sniffiness about Enlightenment, were not rare but rather were 'prevalent within the institution'.

This snapshot is important because it reveals a side to the Islamism-at-Uni problem that's too often overlooked: the failure of academic institutions themselves to confront radical Islamist students and tell them they're talking crap, and more fundamentally their failure to defend rational knowledge and Enlightenment itself. The current obsession with hate preachers, the notion that they're stealing through the academy and corrupting minds, dodges the far bigger problem of intellectual and moral corrosion within the academy itself, the emergence over the past 30 years of a relativistic, 'safe' climate that actively discourages the elevation of any way of thinking over any other and calls into question the value of knowledge itself. If, as Tharoor says, some students 'feel comfortable advocating dangerous and discriminatory beliefs', it will be because they've sussed that they won't be corrected; they know they'll never be told: Kant is better than the Koran.

There's undoubtedly an Islamist problem on campus. I have given numerous talks for Islamic Societies in universities, and I have been pretty disturbed by what I have seen and heard. I've seen row after row of British-born kids trying to look as foreign as possible, the men in smocks (their Nike trainers sticking out the bottom), the women in fashion-conscious veils, the really edgy ones covering up everything but their eyes. It's fashion as fuck-you, where the aim is to appear as ostentatiously non-Western as possible, so that their very presence becomes a challenge to any speaker who was thinking of asserting his secular beliefs over their religious ones. And I've heard these Brits-in-desert-dress argue that freedom is overrated: a packed hall of them laughed when I cited John Stuart Mill on how freedom of choice is the only thing that allows us to assume moral responsibility for our lives. At a debate on Israel, one Muslim student referred to Jews as pigs. The response was amazing: many students said nothing, while others referred to the hate-speech manual in search of the right warning to give him. I just called him an 'anti-Semitic shit', and everyone was taken aback, including the anti-Semite, who, judging by his demeanour, had never been so explicitly called out on his backwardness.

My impression of these students is not that they are spectacularly dangerous—certainly very, very few will become executioners for ISIS—but rather that they are trying their hand, seeing how far they can go in dissing Western ideas and texts and the apparently fake ideals of freedom and rationalism. Their arguments are actually flimsy, and easily laid to waste in debate, but they hold on to them because there's very little pushing back against them. There is no longer a vibrant, confident culture on campus devoted to slaying bad arguments and upholding good ones, to celebrating reason and Enlightened thought, and it is this dearth of Kantian daring, this refusal to assert the academy's own intellectual superiority, which acts as an invitation to students to embrace other ways of thinking, secure in the knowledge that they won't be rebuffed.

As Tharoor says, universities can be 'unwittingly complicit in perpetuating [Islamic] radicalism', through 'allow[ing] Islamist extremism to go unchallenged'. This 'unchallenging' is the key problem. It speaks to what the education writer Joanna Williams describes as a rise in 'anti-Enlightenment' thinking within the academy, where 'academic trends such as critical theory and post-structuralism, as well as political developments within feminism and left-wing politics', have crashed together to create a judgement-dodging climate in which the very idea that any idea is better than another is often called into question.

What's more, students are now told they have the right to exist in a 'safe space', an anti-social, anti-intellectual little world in which no one may challenge their identity or beliefs. A whole

armoury of terms has been invented to shoot down anything that
has the whiff of an intellectual challenge to their 'safety' or self-
esteem. The best-known is 'Islamophobia', which covers, not only
acts of violence against Muslims, but also criticism of Islam. A
recent *Washington Post* piece described how even campus discussions
of jihad and events in the Middle East are now trigger-warned for
'Islamophobia'. There are similar developments here: critique the
beliefs of Islamist students and see how speedily you'll be branded
'Islamophobic'.

Given that their universities often won't stand up for Kant
or Mill or the superiority of rationalism over superstition, and
considering their identities have been ringfenced from ridicule by
various censorious slurs, is it any wonder some students flirt with
non-academic, non-Western ideas? The academy implicitly invites
them to, by sending the message that its own values aren't that
great, and it unwittingly encourages them to hold on to their non-
academic ideas by safe-spacing them from robust critique.

When Cameron and others say we must ban hate preachers,
they're missing the point, and making the problem worse. Rather
than think about how we might re-fortify the academy, and breathe
life back into the Enlightenment side in the battle of ideas, they
avoid the battle of ideas entirely in favour of silencing those who
spout Islamist rubbish. In doing so, they advertise their intellectual
defensiveness, which can only further inflame those students
who already think 'the West' is a hollow, phoney phenomenon.
We should let everyone speak, including the haters, and we should
simultaneously challenge the cult of relativism on campus and
strip away every slur that is now used to silence those who criticise
superstition or stupidity. We should tell students that, with his call on
humanity to grow up, to dare to know, and to use moral reasoning

to impact on the world, Kant is worthy of close and serious study. Kant is better than the Koran. And if they cry Islamophobia? Do that thing with your fingers to signify the playing of the world's smallest violin just for them.

spiked, 2 March 2015

18. TOWARDS A NEW ENLIGHTENMENT

In answer to the question 'What is Enlightenment?', Kant said it was 'man's emergence from his self-imposed nonage'. Nonage isn't a word we use much these days. It means immaturity, childishness, being dependent on others. According to Kant, nonage is 'an inability to use one's own understanding without another's guidance'. And enlightenment, he said, is about emerging from that sad, cushioned, child-like state and 'having the courage to use your own understanding'.

That, in a nutshell, is Enlightenment. We hear a lot of talk these days about there having been 'many Enlightenments' in the 16 and 1700s. And it's true, there were. There was a Scottish Enlightenment, featuring Adam Smith and lots of talk of morality and economics; a French Enlightenment, featuring a lot of blood and cries for liberty and equality; a Dutch Enlightenment, featuring arguments for freedom of speech that still sound radical today: in the 1670s, the Dutch philosopher Baruch Spinoza said 'the liberty of saying what he thinks must be conceded to every man'. Many modern-day politicians should heed that dust-gathering 350-year-old demand.

But boiled down to their essence, these many Enlightenments, all Enlightenment, was about mankind growing up—stepping out of his self-imposed immaturity into the scary but far more interesting world of autonomous adulthood. As Kant said, the motto of the Enlightenment was 'dare to know!'. It was about encouraging individuals to 'use their reason in all matters'.

Well, if that is Enlightenment, we can be pretty certain we now live in un-Enlightened times. For today, far from being encouraged to grow up and strike out, we're being sent back to nonage; back to that nursery of pre-Enlightenment existence, when men and women were presumed to be juvenile, thoughtless creatures in need of constant guidance.

Reading Kant's essay 'What is Enlightenment?' today, more than 200 years after it was first published in 1784, it's remarkable how much his era sounds like the nanny, nagging, nudging states many of us live under today.

Kant bemoaned the fact that the educated echelons of society had 'set themselves up as guardians' of mankind. He wrote: 'I have a book that thinks for me, a pastor who acts as my conscience, a physician who prescribes my diet…' These 'guardians' treat people as 'domestic cattle', he said—they 'carefully prevent the docile creatures from taking a single step without the leading-strings to which they have fastened them'. These interferers have convinced 'the overwhelming majority of mankind' that it should 'consider the step to maturity, not only as hard, but as extremely dangerous', Kant angrily complained.

Doesn't this sound spookily familiar? He could have been writing about 21st-century Britain, or Australia, or America. Because today, once again, we're surrounded by armies of guardians, telling us that to go it alone, to leap headfirst into life without the support of lifestyle gurus and parenting experts and booze-level advisers, is not only hard but extremely dangerous.

It might not be pointy-hatted men of God who now hector us. But we do still have books that think for us, on everything from what to eat to how to raise our kids. We have legions of therapists who emote for us, telling us which emotions are good—self-revelation, self-esteem—and which ones are bad: anger, passion, stoicism. And like poor Kant, we have physicians who prescribe our diets. You can't swing a supersize bar of chocolate these days without hitting 10 experts itching to tell us how much fruit and veg we should eat if we don't want to die early and fat.

Kant didn't like having pastors acting as his conscience. Well, today we have nudgers who aspire to be our 'surrogate willpower'. The Nudge Unit in Downing Street actually uses that phrase— 'surrogate willpower'—to describe its desire to make lifestyle choices on the little people's behalf and then nudge us towards them.

If anything, today's guardians are worse than the moralistic busybodies who infuriated Kant. For now, standing on one's own two feet isn't only discouraged—it's pathologised. If you refuse to kowtow to therapists' diktats, you're 'in denial'. If you get angry, you're told you have 'intermittent explosive disorder'. If you say 'screw you' to the diet prescribers and continue to scoff butter and wine, you'll be told you have a food disorder. Today's guardians have rebranded moral autonomy as a mental illness, convincing their cattle that life on your own isn't just hard—it could kill you.

The rise of new, even more patronising guardians explains why our societies are so anti-freedom. When people aren't trusted to run their own lives, to think and feel and exist without guidance, it's inevitable that more rules will emerge to nag us into doing and thinking what our guardians think we should be doing and thinking. Whether it's hate-speech laws, bans on smoking in public, or petty rules about when adults may engage with children, loads of new laws now govern the minutiae of our lives.

Kant said there was only one sure way to become Enlightened — by being free. He wrote: 'The Enlightenment requires nothing but freedom.' He said that it's only through being free that the human spirit can 'expand to the limit of its capacity'. All the great thinkers of the Enlightenment agreed on the importance of freedom. From John Locke to John Stuart Mill, they all said that to become Enlightened we needed to be free—free to think and to speak as we see fit and to determine our destinies for ourselves.

That's because they trusted in humankind. Unlike the pastors of their time or the nudgers of ours, they believed individuals were capable of governing their own lives. We need to recover that trust in people, and that thirst for freedom. Rebel against the guardians, say no to nudging and lifestyle policing, and let's finally do what Kant suggested we should nearly 250 years ago: 'Walk firmly and cultivate your own mind.'

ABC Radio broadcast, 3 November 2014

19. The return of Fortuna

Fate is making a comeback. The idea that a human being's fortunes are shaped by forces beyond his control is returning, zombie-like, from the graveyard of bad historical ideas. The notion that a man's character and destiny are determined for him rather than by him is back in fashion, after 500-odd years of having been criticised by humanist thinkers.

Of course, we're far too sophisticated these days actually to use the f-word, fate. We don't talk about a god called Fortuna, as the Romans did, believing that this blind, mysterious creature decided people's fates with the spin of a wheel. Unlike long-gone Norse communities we don't believe in goddesses called Norns, who would attend the birth of every child to determine his or her future. No, today we use scientific terms to argue that people's fortunes are determined by higher powers than their little, insignificant selves.

We use and abuse neuroscience to claim certain people are 'born this way'. We claim evolutionary psychology explains why people behave and think the way they do. We use phrases like 'weather of mass destruction', in place of 'gods', to push the idea that mankind is a little thing battered by awesome, destiny-determining forces. Fate has been brought back from the dead and she's been dolled up in pseudoscientific rags.

The intellectual challenge to the idea of fate was one of the most significant things about the Renaissance and the Enlightenment. There had always been an inkling of a belief within mankind that it was possible for individuals to influence their destiny, if not actually shape it. The Romans, for example, believed Fortuna would be kinder to brave, virtuous men. If you did good and took risks you had a better chance of being smiled upon by Fortuna. 'Fortune favours the brave.' But it wasn't until the Renaissance that the idea that men could make their own fortunes really took hold. It's then we see the emergence of the belief that by exercising his free will, a man can become master of his fate.

The earliest texts in Renaissance Italy devoted themselves to questioning the idea that man is the prisoner of a preordained destiny. Francesco Petrarch was one of the first humanists. His 1366 book *Remedies For Fortune Fair and Foul* argued that, alone among God's creatures, mankind has the ability to control his destiny. Giannozzo Manetti, in his 1452 book *On the Dignity and Excellence of Man*, said men could shape their own fates by 'the many operations of intelligence and will'. Also in the 1400s, the Italian scholar Leon Alberti said it was possible for individuals to reach 'the highest pinnacle of glory', even though, as he put it, 'invidious Fortune opposes us'.

In short, mankind is a self-willed, autonomous creature. He's a potentially more powerful force than Fortuna. In the words of the 20th-century philosopher Eugenio Garin, the motif of the Renaissance was this: 'It is always open to men to exercise their virtue in such a way as to overcome the power of Fortuna.'

It's hard to overstate what a radical idea this was at the tailend of the Dark Ages. It's this idea which gives rise to the concept of free will, to the concept of personality even. And it was an idea carried through to the Enlightenment and on to the humanist liberalism of the nineteenth and early 20th centuries. In the words of the greatest liberal, Mill, it is incumbent upon the individual to never 'let the world, or his portion of it, choose his plan of life for him'.

But today, in our downbeat era that bears a passing resemblance to the Dark Ages, we're turning the clock back on this idea. We're rewinding the historic breakthroughs of the Renaissance and Enlightenment, and we're breathing life back into the fantasy of fate. Ours is an era jampacked with deterministic theories, claims that human beings are like amoeba in a Petri dish being prodded and shaped by various forces. But the new determinism isn't religious or supernatural, as it was in the pre-Enlightened era—it's scientific determinism, or rather pseudo-scientific determinism.

There's neuro-determinism, the idea that we're fundamentally products of the accidental shape or chemical liveliness of our brains. Everything from our criminal instincts to our musical giftedness to our political orientation is now said to have been bestowed on us by the grey matter in our heads. A recent study on the 'neurobiology of politics' claimed that whether a person becomes a liberal or a conservative depends on his 'brain circuits', particularly the circuits that deal with conflict. So now, we can't even choose our political outlook, apparently; we're not even in control of our voting destinies.

Then there's evolutionary determinism, the idea that we're compelled by what one author calls our 'evolutionary wiring'. We're told that our passion for consumerism is an evolutionary trait, a product of our 'primitive, instinctive brains', in the words of green writer John Naish, which drive us to 'get more of everything, whenever possible'. Some experts even claim there's a 'rapist gene', another byproduct of natural evolution and the instinctive urge of men to procreate. Once again, the ability of mankind to make moral judgements about his behaviour, to be the author of his life, is undermined by the idea that we're hardwired to behave a particular way.

There's also the rising trend of infant determinism. So-called 'early years' theory claims that a person's life fortunes are determined by whether his mother breastfeeds him, his father reads to him, how much he's cuddled, and so on. Books with titles like *Why Love Matters: How Affection Shapes a Baby's Brain* claim that bad parenting can inflict 'lifelong handicaps' on children. In short, every mum and dad is a mini-Fortuna, and all of us are apparently just the damaged end products of what our parents said and did to us. We're not the shapers of our own characters but rather are creatures whose fates were sealed by others before we hit the age of five.

And of course there's environmental determinism, the trend for personifying the weather and the sea and the air, depicting them as god-like thwarters of human fortunes. Green determinism most closely resembles the old, pre-modern belief in gods of fortune. So in response to floods and other strange weather events, a respected British environmentalist has written: 'From the storm clouds, the hand of God reaches down, clutching a large piece of paper labelled "the bill".' In other words, Nature, godlike and furious, is exacting her revenge on rampaging mankind.

These modern determinisms are worse than the old pre-modern belief in fate. At least ancient communities, like the Romans, believed that by being brave and virtuous an individual could offset the harshest judgements of the gods of fortune. The new determinism offers no such scope for the exercise of bravery or autonomy. Instead it demands that we be meek and apologetic in the face of awesome powers like angry nature. It demands that we accept that tiny cliques of experts—whether brain-scanners, parenting gurus or climatologists—are the only ones who can reveal to us our fate and advise us on how to prepare for its inevitable playing out. It tells us we're not really the subjects of history, but the objects of history, tossed about by this and that powerful force.

In such a stifling climate, we could do with a new Renaissance. We could do with declaring a war of words on today's fatalistic experts just as surely as the scholars of the Renaissance stood up to invidious Fortuna. We could do with asserting the ability of human beings, through the exercise of free will and the deployment of their moral autonomy, to shape their futures. We could do with speaking up once again for 'the dignity and excellence of man'.

ABC Radio broadcast, 14 January 2014

20. THE MULTICULTURAL CONCEIT

If Europe really wants to pay tribute to the massacred *Charlie Hebdo* staff, it could do worse than ditch the term 'Islamophobia'. For this cynical phrase, this multicultural conceit, has done an untold amount to promote the idea that ridiculing other people's beliefs and cultures is a bad thing. In fact, the widely used but little thought-on i-word has pathologised the very act of making a judgement. It has turned the totally legitimate conviction that some belief systems are inferior to others into a swirling, irrational fear—a phobia—worthy of condemnation and maybe even investigation by officials. That those two gunmen thought *Charlie Hebdo*'s 'Islamophobic' cartoonists deserved punishment isn't surprising: they grew up on a continent so riven by relativism that even saying 'Islamic values are not as good as Enlightenment values' is now treated as evidence of a warped, sinful mind, as a crime, effectively, to be punished.

Rarely has the disconnect between the claims of the Islamophobia industry and the reality on the ground in Europe been as starkly exposed as it was following the slaughter at *Charlie Hebdo*. The cartoonists' spilt blood was still warm when, moving on with callous speed from this act of barbarism, the respectable media started fretting about the danger now faced by European Muslims. We should all fear 'the coming Islamophobic backlash', said one hack. But no Pavlovian backlash came. The unreality of the Islamophobia industry's claims became startlingly clear following the murder of four Jews in a shop by an accomplice of the *Charlie Hebdo* killers. Even after this act of anti-Semitism, observers continued to fret about the mortal threat allegedly facing Muslims. As the bodies of the four Jews were being prepared for the flight to Israel, George Clooney was telling fawning reporters how worried he was about 'anti-Muslim fervour' in Europe. It's surreal; real through-the-looking-glass stuff.

The factual chasm between the fears of the Islamophobia panickers and what actually happens after a terrorist attack reveals a seldom-grasped truth about the idea of Islamophobia: it is not in fact a description of any rise in racist thinking; rather, it is a term that developed and spread to chastise the moral criticism of certain belief systems. The now Europe-wide concern about Islamophobia differs from all other modern campaigns against prejudice in one important way: it is the creation of political elites rather than being a grassroots campaign to win equality or liberty for a particular minority. Islamophobia is a multicultural conceit, the invention of infinitesimally small, aloof, crisis-ridden elites keen to clamp down on any heated or overly judgmental discussion of non-Western values.

Unlike the civil rights movement in 1950s and 1960s America, where vast numbers of blacks fought tooth-and-nail against racial segregation and state violence, the concern with Islamophobia came not from the streets but from the rarefied world of think-tanks and professional handwringers. The current understanding of 'Islamophobia' comes in large part from a 1996 report produced by the Runnymede Trust, a UK-based race-equality think-tank. This report's definition of Islamophobia—'a shorthand way of referring to the dread or hatred of Islam'—is now the most widely accepted, not only in Britain but in much of Europe. Tellingly, the Runnymede report was based, not on any serious measurement of real-world discrimination against Muslims, but predominantly on an analysis of the media depiction of Islam and its followers.

That is, from the very outset the term Islamophobia was more concerned with media and moral judgement of a belief system—with apparently problematic *words* and *ideas*—than it was with actual physical or institutionalised prejudice against Muslims.

Even more tellingly, 3,500 copies of the report were distributed among, as one author describes it, 'metropolitan authorities, race-equality councils, police forces, government departments, unions, professional associations, think tanks and universities'. The great and good. These were to be the watchers for any expression of 'dread of Islam', the policers, in essence, of criticism of a belief system.

The Runnymede report makes clear the key concern of those who invented the idea of Islamophobia: that it's wrong to be judgmental of non-Western values or to elevate the West's way of life over other ways of life. As this defining document puts it, one sure sign of 'Islamophobia' is a view of Islam as 'inferior to the West'. In order to challenge Islamophobia, Runnymede suggested to the cliques of academics, coppers and officials it sent its report to that they should encourage people to understand that Islam is 'distinctively different, but not deficient' and is 'as equally worthy of respect [as Western values]'. Furthermore, it said, we brave warriors against Islamophobia must challenge the idea that Islam's criticisms of the West are without foundation and should instead encourage people to consider and embrace '[Islam]'s criticism of "the West" and other cultures'.

What we have here is not any traditional campaign against racism, but rather a censorious assault on certain ways of thinking, on moral judgment itself. In chastising the belief that Islam might not be as great as what are called 'Western values' (shorthand for the universal ideals of democracy and liberty), and insisting that

Islam is in fact worthy of 'equal respect', the Runnymede report was designed to promote relativism and self-censorship, not equality or social progress.

This cynical use of the 'phobia' brand to harry and even criminalise anyone who argues that secularism and freedom are better than the Islamic outlook has grown since 1996. Now, everything from expressing disdain for the burqa to blaspheming against Muhammad is described as 'Islamophobic', as deserving of opprobrium. This can be seen in the constant branding as 'Islamophobic' commentators who simply criticise aspects of Islam. So in recent years, European race watchdogs have reprimanded journalists for describing the Koran as providing 'scriptural cover for judicial barbarity' and even slammed the BBC for describing Osama bin Laden as an 'Islamic fundamentalist', on the basis that actually his acts were 'un-Islamic'. So even pointing out the religious origins of certain terrorists is seen as 'Islamophobic'.

And of course, this is what *Charlie Hebdo* was in recent years slammed for doing, by everyone from Barack Obama to French politicians and courts: expressing a morally superior viewpoint about Islam. We have created a climate in which criticising Islam is seen as foul, racist, mentally deranged, and then we wonder why some Islamic hotheads seek to punish those who dare to do it. The *Charlie Hebdo* murderers are the armed wing of the Islamophobia industry: it was the European elite that made criticism of Islam a crime, and those two gunmen who punished that crime with summary execution.

The conceit of Islamophobia is at the cutting edge of the ideology of multiculturalism. Multiculturalism embodies the modern West's reluctance to elevate any culture, even its own, above any other.

Multiculturalism makes a virtue of a moral vacuum, turning the negative inability of the modern West to say 'Our way of life is good' into a pseudo-positive celebration of all cultures as 'equally worthy of respect'. Multiculturalism is about evading any serious discussion of values or ideas in favour of saying 'all are good, none should be ridiculed'. The idea of Islamophobia takes this to the next level, through demonising the very desire to judge. Far from a progressive war on racism, the Islamophobia industry is a deeply illiberal attempt to squash debate, and to sneak rules against blasphemy back into Europe.

But we must be free to blaspheme. And to ridicule. And, most importantly, to discuss and judge and discriminate between values we think are good and those we think are less good. Western societies will never rediscover their sense of purpose or mission, far less the Enlightenment spirit, so long as the very act of bigging up one's own democratic and liberal values over the views of others is treated as tantamount to a speech crime. 'Je suis Charlie'? Then challenge the very thing that contributed to the massacre of those Charlies: the stifling new culture of relativism and self-censorship that has given some people in Europe the foolish and dangerous idea that they have the right to go through life without ever hearing a sore word about their belief system.

spiked, 13 January 2015

21. THE VAGINA VOTERS

'I intend to vote with my vagina.'

Have you ever read a more squirm-inducing sentence than that? It appeared in a pro-Hillary piece in *Dame* magazine, written by a person with a vagina who intends to vote for Clinton because she also has a vagina.

Let's leave aside the unfortunate image conjured up by that sentence ('You can hold a pencil with that thing?!'). The bigger problem with such unabashed declarations of 'vagina voting' is that they confirm the descent of feminism into the cesspool of identity politics, even biologism, and its abandonment of the idea that women should be valued more for their minds than their anatomy.

Kate Harding, the vagina voter in question, isn't only going to vote with her vag—she's also going to tell everyone about it. 'I intend to vote with my vagina. Unapologetically. Enthusiastically … And I intend to talk about it', she wrote in *Dame*. She thinks Hillary would be a great president because she 'knows what it's like to menstruate, be pregnant, [and] give birth'.

So you're going to pick your leader on the basis of her biological functions, the fact she's experienced the same bodily stuff as you? Imagine if a man did that. 'I'm voting for Ted Cruz because he knows what it's like to jack off. And he knows the pain of being kicked in the balls.' We'd think that was a very sad dude indeed. Why is it any better for a female commentator to wax lyrical about voting on the basis of her biological similarity to a candidate rather than any shared political outlook?

The point of Harding's pussy politics, as I think we should call this biologism among some in the Hillary camp, is to say that it would be a brilliant, symbolic breakthrough if the US were to have its first-ever female president. It would be 'enormously important,' she says. 'American women have been bleeding for over 200 years'—again with the blood!—'and a lot of us have arrived at the point where we just want someone with a visceral, not abstract, concept of what that means.'

There's something profoundly sexist in this. Hillary is valued, not for her ability to think abstractly, which is the very essence of politics, but for what she represents viscerally—the visceral being, in the words of the *Oxford English Dictionary*, the bowels, 'the seat of emotion'.

A hundred years ago, the precise same view of women as visceral rather than abstract creatures was used as an argument against having them in the political realm. In 1910, the London-based journal *The Anti-Suffrage Review* said women have difficulty 'forming abstract ideas'. 'Woman is emotional', it said, 'and government by emotion quickly degenerates into injustice'. Yet now, a century later, the potential first woman president of the US is hailed by some for her visceral—'not abstract', in Harding's words—understanding of women's lives and everyday issues. To stick with the biological-function theme, modern feminism is pooping all over the Suffragettes, who fought tooth-and-nail against the valuation of their viscera over their brains.

Harding's pussy politics is only a more physical, blood-obsessed version of one of the main arguments coming from Hillary's cheerleaders in the media: that she deserves to be elected because she's a woman, because she has a vagina.

In response to the claim that Hillary is 'playing the gender card', feminist author Jessica Valenti says 'good', adding 'I hope she plays the gender card so hard'. Valenti writes about 'the very important, symbolic and necessary vision of the first woman president', and says 'that's a gender card I'd play again and again'. In short, she's voting with her vagina.

Chelsea Clinton says her mother's femaleness is 'absolutely important for … symbolic reasons'. Nancy Pelosi says Hillary's sex should be a 'very major consideration' for voters, because of the brilliant gravity of 'what it would mean to elect a woman president of the United States'. In short, vote with your vaginas. Or if you're in the unfortunate position of having a dick, then at least give 'very major consideration' to the fact that Hillary is a woman and vote for her accordingly. Think about what is in this woman's knickers rather than what is in her mind.

Over at *Bustle* magazine, Gabrielle Moss continues the Suffragette-defaming fashion for elevating women's biology over their brains, admitting she will be 'voting with my emotions' and eschewing the 'clear-eyed political rationality that so many of the men around me [claim] to possess'. She says her vote for Clinton won't be 'based on a clear-eyed, unemotional review of her political track record', nor on a 'clear-eyed assessment of all possible Democratic candidates', but rather will be an expression of the 'intense personal connection' she feels with Hillary as a woman. They both have vaginas, you see.

Here, again, the very thing the Suffragettes street-fought against—the idea that women are too emotional to partake in abstract politics—is bizarrely rehabilitated as a badge of honour. I'm a woman, and therefore I'm visceral, and I will vote for a woman. Vaginas of the World, Unite!

The rise of vagina voting, and the centrality of gender to the whole Hillary shebang, shows how dominant the politics of identity has become in the space of just eight years. Back in 2007/2008, Hillary bristled at the idea that she should big-up her gender and make a major display of her femaleness. 'I'm not running as a woman', she told an audience in Iowa. Now, however, she is running as a woman—selling herself as a grandmother, peppering her campaign launch video with women of every age and hue— and she's celebrated for doing so.

In 2008 she 'struggled against the idea' that she was representing a particular gender, says the *Guardian*, among the Clinton family's most fawning fans, but this time she's putting 'gender at the forefront of her presidential race', the paper's coverage says, approvingly. Or as one news report put it: 'Ms Clinton played down the gender role the first time she ran for the top job. But this time it's expected to be a core plank of her campaign.'

This embrace of the gender card by Clinton and her cronies, this move from thinking with their heads to voting with their vaginas, is being celebrated as a great leap forward. It's nothing of the sort. It merely confirms the speedy and terrifying shrinking of the political sphere in recent years, with the abstract being elbowed aside by the emotional, and the old focus on ideas and values now playing a very quiet second fiddle to an obsession with identity.

The celebration of a potential president on the basis of her natural characteristics shows that the growing vacuum where big and serious ideas ought to be is being filled with biologism, with a view of people as little more than bundles of genes, accidents of birth, colours, sexes, genders. The rotten thing that human beings struggled against for generations—the tendency to judge

individuals by their biology rather than their talents and beliefs —
has made a comeback under the banner of identity politics.

In 2001, *The Onion* did one of its brilliant 'American Voices'
polls on the question of Hillary standing for the presidency in
2004. One of the respondents, the white guy in the suit, says: 'A
woman president? What if she menstruates all over some important
legislation?' So as recently as 2001, talking about Hillary as someone
who menstruates was recognised to be a sexist throwback to
that old, dark era when women were treated as animalistic, and
not as capable of abstract reasoning as men; today, the fact that
Hillary 'knows what it's like to menstruate' is presented as a serious
reason to vote for her. Meet the vagina voters, the new sexists,
reducing women to bits of flesh as thoroughly as those hoary old
misogynists were doing a hundred years ago.

Reason, 3 May 2015

22. Barry Spurr's soul

Why is it bad to hack and expose photographs of a woman's naked body but okay to steal and make public the contents of a man's soul? This question should burn in our minds following the Barry Spurr scandal.

When a hacker invaded the iCloud accounts of female celebs and rifled through their intimate snaps, there was global outrage. This theft of explicit private photos of actress Jennifer Lawrence and others was a sex crime, we were told. It was an act of misogynistic tyranny, proof that even women's private lives are not safe from the bulging eyes and clasping hands of a hateful, macho culture.

Fast forward a few weeks, and some of the same people whose jaws hit the floor at the audacity of those who leaked those women's private, unguarded pics were cheering the hacking of Spurr's private, unguarded words.

Spurr, a professor of poetry at the University of Sydney, had his private emails pored over and published by left-miserabilist website *New Matilda*. In some of his emails, in what he later claimed was a cheeky competition between him and his friends to see who could be the least PC, Spurr used words that would no doubt cause pinot gris to be spilled if they were uttered at a dinner party. He described Tony Abbott as an 'Abo lover', referred to a woman as a 'harlot', called Nelson Mandela a 'darky', and used 'Mussies' for Muslims. He was suspended by the university.

Many people will wince upon reading those words. Just as we will have winced if we happened upon those photos of well-known women doing porno poses. And that's because these behaviours, both Spurr's knowingly outrageous banter and the actresses' knowingly sluttish poses, share something important in common: they were private acts, not intended for us. They were things done or said between intimates, far from the eyes and ears of respectable society. Yet where right-on commentators and tweeters stood up for the right of famous women not to have their private nakedness splashed across the internet, they relished the exposure of Spurr's soul to the eyes of the world.

Spurr's private thoughts are fair game for public ridicule, they said, because of his position as a specialist consultant to the federal government's review of the national curriculum. *New Matilda* said Spurr's standing as someone who could 'influence what will be taught to every child in every school' means his intimate chatter is a legitimate target for moral policing. His private thoughts clash with his public duties, it said.

Imagine if this tyrannical insistence that everyone should have a spotless private life were taken to its logical conclusion. For a start, we might argue that it was legit to leak those female celebs' intimate photos on the grounds that they exposed the women's hypocrisy. Many of these actresses and singers are role models to young girls and pose as demure creatures in their work lives. But behind closed doors they get up to stuff that wouldn't look out of place in *Hustler*. Their private lives run counter to their public personas. Does that mean they should be exposed, mocked, ridiculed? Of course not. And neither should Spurr.

No amount of faux-progressive lingo about exposing 'institutional racism' in the upper echelons of Australian society can disguise the fact that Spurr-bashing was an old-fashioned, McCarthyite hounding of someone for having a private life and private thoughts that fail to adhere to new orthodoxies.

New Matilda gave the game away when it said it had one aim—
'cleansing the national curriculum review of the toxicity of this
man's views'. Cleansing. What a word. It speaks to the true driving
force behind the assaults on Spurr: an authoritarian instinct to rid
the public realm of anyone whose outlook is not 100 per cent pure
and decent, as defined by the new self-styled guardians of moral
probity: so-called progressives, with righteousness in their hearts
and rotten tomatoes in their hands.

We need to face up to the seriousness, the sheer intolerance,
of the creeping new trend for punishing people for their private
thoughts. In the US, Donald Sterling, a business magnate and
owner of the Los Angeles Clippers basketball team, was expelled
from basketball and turned into an object of international ridicule
following the leaking of an entirely private phone conversation
in which he said something disrespectful about black people. In
Britain, two football managers were sacked following the leaking
of private emails in which they made juvenile jokes about gays and
black people. And then came (and went) Spurr.

There is something Stasi-like in this moral policing of private
speech. In the wake of the Sterling scandal, a columnist for
the *Washington Post* said: 'If you don't want your words broadcast in
the public square, don't say them … Such potential exposure forces
us to more carefully select our words and edit our thoughts.'

This is terrifying. It is a straight-up celebration of the kind of
public denunciations of private deviancy that were encouraged
under Stalinist regimes. Why don't we just put a *Nineteen Eighty-
Four*-style telescreen in everyone's homes? That's surely the only
way to ensure that no one misspeaks privately, and instead edits
their thoughts and suppresses their more 'toxic views'.

The haranguing of Spurr and other private speakers turns the clock back to a darker moment in human history. During the Inquisition, people were regularly tried and punished for their private beliefs. The Enlightenment thinkers who came in the wake of that calamity insisted that such tyranny should stop. In the words of the great enlightened 17th-century English jurist Edward Coke: 'No man, ecclesiastical or temporal, shall be examined upon the secret thoughts of his heart, or of his secret opinion.' Spurr was punished for his secret opinion.

Coke's enlightened view, his conviction that individuals must be free to think and say what they want in their private lives, is in mortal danger today. It's being crushed by a New Inquisition, staffed by members of the chattering classes, inflamed by Twitter and assaulting not only individuals like Spurr but also the very principles of privacy, autonomy and freedom of thought.

The Australian, 25 October 2014

23. THE HUMANITY OF FUR

The fashion industry is famously fickle. Ten years ago, supermodels were getting their kits off and tits out for anti-fur adverts. Today some of the same models wear dead foxes, tail and all, slung over their shoulders, or the fur of aborted lamb fetuses (seriously).

Meanwhile, those who foolishly thought that the earlier anti-fur stance was more than a fad are furious. People for the Ethical Treatment of Animals (PETA), the ferocious animal libbers, has denounced Jennifer Lopez as 'Fur Scum' for including rabbit-trimmed jackets in her clothing line, and scolded Elizabeth Jagger for wearing a fox at London Fashion Week.

I stand with the fur-wearers. The anti-fur movement is motivated by base anthropomorphism, a belief that animals are humans' equals. And to that, humanists should say: there is no greater privilege for an animal, which otherwise would scurry around, eat, shit, breed and then die, than to be made into a fur coat, which can be worn and admired for generations.

Animal-rights activists say the fur industry is cruel, causing pain and distress to innocent animals. 'How would you like it?', they ask, as captured in an anti-fur TV ad which showed a woman in a fancy fur being accosted by burly men, clubbed around the head, and stripped of her coat. The implication is that a mink experiences being hunted exactly as the sexy broad who ends up wearing said mink would experience it.

Yet according to Stuart Derbyshire, an expert in the neurophysiology of pain at the University of Pittsburgh, the fact that an animal might scream or recoil when trapped doesn't show that it has an appreciation of pain. 'Chop the head off a chicken and it will continue to run around. If you catch the headless chicken—quickly!—and stick a pin in its foot, it will still flinch, despite no longer having a head or a brain', he says. 'These reflex responses are coordinated by a spinal-motor loop and do not involve the brain or require conscious experience.'

It is different for humans—and profoundly so. A beast runs away out of an instinct for survival, bestowed on it by the evolutionary process. A human, with his self-awareness, his consciousness, would leg it from a knife-wielding hunter from a dire appreciation of what being skinned alive and killed would entail—for himself, his future, his family and friends. A hunted human might think to himself 'I could die today', and what a terrifying thought that would be! An animal is incapable of thinking 'I could die today', as Derbyshire explains: 'Animals do not understand the concept of "today", unless we think foxes use calendars and keep diaries; or "die", unless we think that mink have funeral rites; or "could", because they have no sense of probabilistic inference; or even "I", because they also have no sense of self.' Such concepts, says Derbyshire, are 'uniquely human'.

So while the physical responses of a human and an animal to being hunted look similar, they couldn't be more different. The difference is in the screaming. PETA's bunnies that 'scream' at the prospect of being made into a jacket for Ms Lopez do so only instinctively, to grab the attention of a parent or other member of the group. A human scream in similar circumstances would be infinitely more deathly, expressing fear, angst, a horrible appreciation of what is about to occur.

Of course, animals should be treated humanely, even in the

run-up to having their fur pulled off. But the animal libbers want more than humane treatment—they want animals to be treated as equal to us. And, scarily, this childish attitude toward animals is no longer the preserve of radical vegans who shout abuse at J-Lo—it increasingly informs public debate on important matters of scientific endeavour. A Working Party of the British Nuffield Council on Bioethics, a serious scientific body, said in a recent report on the ethics of animal research that it rejected the idea of 'categorical human superiority' over animals. Even serious thinkers are buying into today's bizarre, *Bambi*-inspired worldview of animal-and-human sameness.

The idea that we are morally superior to animals is not some pose; it is the foundation of human civilisation. And the attack on that idea of superiority today, by the anti-fur movement, anti-vivisectionists and others, and the distaste for it even at the highest levels of government and science, represents an attack on our civilisation.

In such circumstances, we should defend fashionistas from the anti-fur lot, and point to the humanising side of the fur industry. To turn an animal into a fur coat is to ennoble it. As a fashion item, an animal acquires a significance far beyond its own natural existence. Indeed, the only true 'purpose' in the life of a mink or rabbit is that bestowed on it by the hunter, skinner and fur-maker. Through their efforts, an animal is elevated from an instinct-driven bundle of reflex responses to an item worthy of being displayed in Paris, London and New York. Through human endeavour and labour an animal is given a use and meaning nature could never have designed for it. What is a fox but a wild dog scrabbling for food on the forest floor, destined to die and rot in a dirthole? The fox worn by Jagger was spared this fate and made into something memorably beautiful.

No finer fate can befall an animal than to be caught by a fur-hunter. And if they 'scream' it's only because they are too dumb to realise that.

Reason, 10 October 2005

24. THE HUMAN HEART

How's this for heartening: the number of people in Europe dying from heart disease has more than halved since the 1980s. In almost every EU country there has been a 'dramatic drop' in death by cardiovascular disease, said a study published in the *European Heart Journal*. Among both women and men (yes, even blokes), and among every age group, including the over-65s, there has been a 'large and significant decrease in death rates from heart disease', said the study. If anything deserves a 'Wow', it's these findings.

In a nutshell: in the space of one generation, in the time it took for Madonna to go from singing 'Holiday' to adopting black babies from Africa, mankind has won some massive, tide-turning battles in the war on heart disease. Which is really a war on nature—on capricious nature's failure to provide us with hearts that can withstand all the crap we throw at them, from physical exertion to fatty foods to emotional stress.

Even in the US, which some Europeans have a sniffy tendency to look upon as a land of elephantine eating habits and corresponding bodily rot, heart disease is in retreat from humanity's scalpel-waving charge: there's been 'a substantial, persistent and remarkable decline in deaths from heart disease' in the US, as one study puts it. In every year since 1968, heart-disease death rates in the US have fallen. In 2012, around 600,000 Americans died from heart disease; sad, yes—but if the death rate had remained at its 1968 levels, closer to 1.5 million would have died.

Mankind's creeping victory over heart disease is, ultimately, a story of targeted human endeavour, of scientific and technological discoveries conspiring to do away with one of the major ailments that prevents people from living full, long lives. Anti-smoking moral entrepreneurs, adept at hogging the headlines, insist heart-disease death rates are falling because people are giving up cigarettes. In truth, it's a combination of medical and technological breakthroughs—from the development of various heart-fortifying drugs to the invention of machines that keep pumping blood around the body during surgery on the heart—that has led to such a dramatic diminution in heart suffering. Consider heart bypass surgery, developed in the 1960s, where veins from one part of a person's body are grafted on to his sick heart in order to 'bypass' its narrowed veins. 'Bypass'—I love that word, for this intricate surgery, like all human technological endeavour, is really a bypassing of nature and its whims and idiocies.

And yet, the revelation about a generational plummeting in heart-disease death rates in Europe was not greeted as a victory for man over sickness. There was no substantial coverage of it at all. In fact, in the same week it came out it was dwarfed by news reports about how being overweight by just four pounds can increase our risk of heart disease. We had the extraordinary situation where a report revealing humanity's inspired reversing of the rot that afflicts many a human heart was demoted by familiar scaremongering about heart disease.

There are two reasons for this incapacity to cheer the shrinking of heart-disease deaths. The first is that modern-day moral crusaders can never admit they've won. They can never openly say that the object of their fury – whether it's disease, malnutrition or child destitution—is finally being consigned to the dustbin of history. For to do so would rob them of their *raison d'être*, which is to moralise at the masses. And so they carry on scaremongering, even as human life improves all the time.

The second, more important reason why revelations about the halving of heart-disease deaths passed almost unnoticed is because ours is an era that isn't well disposed to stories of human ingenuity. Ours is an era in which very few mull over what a Renaissance scholar called 'the dignity and excellence of man', and very many view human beings as toxic, polluting, destructive creatures, adept at ruining both their own lives and the world around them. We're far more comfortable with the image of human beings as fat destroyers of their own hearts than as enlightened, reasoned warriors against disease, natural limits, and all the other things that have the temerity to try to hold us back. It's the biggest problem we face in our technologically buzzing but morally defeatist young millennium: the dearth of faith in humankind, the treatment of man as a rampaging bovine creature rather than as what he is: the only conscious force on this planet, who has more than demonstrated his capacity to extend and improve human existence and to tame his wild, unforgiving surroundings.

For millennia, long before the dawn of science, human communities were in awe of the heart. They knew there was something beating in the chest, and that if it stopped beating, we died. The heart came to symbolise everything vital and urgent about human beings; it was seen as the source of virtue, love, bravery. How fitting that today, when such human values are held in profoundly low esteem, the heart is now more likely to be depicted as a kind of fleshy grenade, liable to explode at any moment under pressure from an individual's own thoughtless behaviour.

In truth, though, the human heart is stronger than ever, thanks to the work of human brains and hands. And just imagine what we could do against social pathologies as well as physical ones if we put our minds to it, and our hearts were in it.

spiked, 2 July 2013

25. A DUTY TO OFFEND

Speech to the Oxford Union

Seven hundred years ago, if someone had come to Oxford and stood here and said, 'I think everyone should be allowed to read the Bible, even peasants', that person would have been described as offensive. He would have been denounced, shouted at, and eventually no-platformed.

That was certainly the experience of John Wycliffe. In 1382 he was banished from Oxford for, among other things, translating the Bible into English. His work was described as an offence against the ecclesiastical order.

Two hundred years ago, if someone had come to Oxford and stood here and said, 'I don't believe in God', that person would have been described as offensive. He would have been ridiculed, yelled at.

That was certainly the experience of Shelley, who in 1811 was banished from Oxford for writing a pamphlet called *The Necessity of Atheism.*

One historical account describes how Shelley's pamphlet caused 'maximum offence'. It describes how fellows and students at New College 'swept the pamphlets up' and disposed of them—much like today's student leaders sweep up lads' mags, which they also describe as causing 'maximum offence'.

One hundred years ago, if someone had come to Oxford and stood here and said, 'I think a man should be allowed to have sex with another man', that person would have been described as offensive. He would have been booed, hissed at, no-platformed.

That was certainly the experience of *The Chameleon*, an openly gay Oxford magazine which in 1894 survived for one issue only. Why? Because it was offensive. One observer called it 'an insult to the animal creation'; there was talk of it having a 'dangerous influence on the young'.

In other words, it made Oxford an unsafe space, and therefore it had to be stopped—much as today's student leaders ban tabloid newspapers in the name of preserving safe spaces for students.

So when today's student leaders clamp down on offensive stuff, they're actually carrying on a very long tradition. A tradition whereby the creme de la creme of British society takes it upon themselves to police the parameters of acceptable thought, to patrol the outskirts of right and proper thinking, and to outlaw offensiveness in the academy.

Throughout history, the church, politicians, universities and various moral movements have always branded certain ideas 'offensive' and have waged war against them. Today, supposedly radical student leaders do the same. They carry out one of the oldest, foulest forms of intolerance—intolerance of those who give offence.

But giving offence is good—it is essential, in fact. Humans have long had the urge to offend against the natural order, the religious order, the moral order, and in the process they have pushed humanity forward.

In fact, pretty much every leap forward in history, pretty much every freedom and comfort we enjoy, is a product of individuals having given offence, having offended against the orthodoxies of their age. Offensiveness is not just something we have to begrudgingly accept—offensiveness is the very motor of human progress.

Copernicus offended Christians with his assertion that the Sun was at the centre of the solar system. He really hurt some of them. And in the process he made the world a better, more understandable place.

John Wilkes, the 18th-century radical journalist, offended everyone. He packed his newspapers not only with political commentary but also with sex and lies and tales of bishops buggering their maids. And in the process, through his struggles with the authorities, he gave birth to press freedom.

The newspaper *Gay News* caused profound offence to Christians in 1976 when it published a poem about a Roman centurion fellating Christ. And in the process, in its struggles with the authorities, it started a debate about the blasphemy laws that would eventually contribute to their abolition—expanding freedom of speech for you and me and everyone.

The right to offend is not some pesky little part of freedom of speech that we have to put up with — it is the heart and soul and lungs of freedom of speech. It is the coursing lifeblood of human progress. It is the instigator of liberty and modernity and science and understanding.

What a laughing stock today's student leaders are, that they can so casually dismiss the right to be offensive without realising that their lovely, enlightened lives are the gift of individuals who gave offence; the gift of scientists, thinkers, agitators who bravely showed their arses to the dominant ideas of their eras. Their offensiveness made you free.

I know what some student leaders will say: 'Oh, but our no-platforming is only about protecting individuals, not ideologies. We only want to protect women from misogyny and black students from racism, so our intolerance is progressive.'

Please. How progressive is it to suggest that female students are so fragile that they can't cope with seeing a pair of tits in *The Sun*? Because that doesn't sound progressive to me—it sounds paternalistic.

How progressive is it to say black students need these wise, white student leaders to protect them from harmful ideas? Because that doesn't sound progressive to me—it sounds neo-colonialist.

The fact is, today's student leaders aren't protecting individuals—they're protecting an idea, and it's the most mainstream, status quo, *bad* idea of the 21st century.

It's the idea of inherent human weakness and incapacity; the poisonous notion that humans are fragile and therefore our speech and our interactions with each other must be monitored and policed and always checked for danger. It is this utterly orthodox, misanthropic idea that they promote, and protect from criticism, just as surely as priests once ringfenced their beliefs from ridicule.

In this choking, censorious climate, where everything is treated as potentially offensive and all sorts of people are no-platformed or safe-spaced into silence, we've got to move beyond talking about a right to offend—we have to talk about a duty to offend.

Anyone who cares for freedom and truth, anyone who believes that humanity only progresses through being daring and sometimes disrespectful, now has a duty to rile and stir and outrage; a duty to break out of the new grey conformism; a duty to ridicule these new guardians of decency; a duty to tell them: 'Fuck your orthodoxies.'

Oxford, 5 March 2015

SPIKED, edited by Brendan O'Neill, was launched in 2001. It was Britain's first online-only current-affairs magazine. While much has changed since then, one thing remains the same: *spiked* continues to stand apart. It's sassy where others are downbeat, irreverent where others conform, and committed to excellence where others dumb down. In no other publication will you find such a heady brew of politics and culture, shot through with an unswerving commitment to making sense of the world.

spiked wears its passions on its editorial sleeve. It is a fan of reason, liberty and progress, and not so keen on panic-mongering, illiberalism and nostalgia. It's the magazine that puts the case for human endeavour, intellectual risk-taking, exploration, excellence in learning and art, and freedom of speech with no ifs and buts, against the myriad miserabilists who would seek to wrap humans in red tape and dampen down our daring. It lives by the motto, 'questioning everything'—or as the *New York Times* put it, '*spiked* is the often-biting British publication fond of puncturing all manner of ideological balloons'.

Start reading *spiked* today, and sign up for our weekly newsletter, at: www.spiked-online.com

Lightning Source UK Ltd.
Milton Keynes UK
UKOW01f0637160217
294549UK00001B/44/P